How to coach
HOCKEY

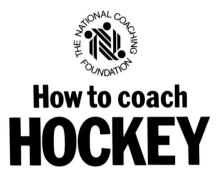

How to coach
HOCKEY

John Law

WILLOW BOOKS

Willow Books
William Collins Sons & Co Ltd
London • Glasgow • Sydney • Auckland
Toronto • Johannesburg

First published 1990

Copyright © William Collins Sons & Co Ltd 1990

A CIP catalogue record for this book is available from the British Library.

ISBN 0 00 218324 2 (paperback)
ISBN 0 00 218373 0 (hardback)

Commissioning Editor: Michael Doggart
Senior Editor: Lynne Gregory
Designer: Peter Laws
Illustrator: Simon Roulstone

This book was designed and produced by
Amanuensis Books Ltd
12 Station Road
Didcot
Oxfordshire
OX11 7LL

Printed in China

The pronoun 'he' has been used throughout and should be
interpreted as applying equally to men and women as appropriate.
It is important in sport, as elsewhere, that women and men should
have equal status and opportunities.

CONTENTS

FOREWORD

John Law is one of the most enthusiastic and dedicated coaches in the game of hockey, and many players have benefitted from his thorough and caring coaching style. I have been privileged to work alongside John on many occasions during the last fifteen years, and watch his methods succeed time and time again - particularly with very young players. He has educated players at all levels of the game from primary school to international, and has built up an enormous reservoir of knowledge.

The fact that he has found time to give the rest of the coaching world the benefit of his experience is testament to both his organization and his desire to contribute to the game.

The ideas, concepts and practices put forward in this book come from a man who has spent over twenty years designing, formulating and modifying his approach; it is typically generous that he should offer the rest of us a shorter route.

Hockey has a great deal going for it at the present time, and I thoroughly recommend coaches to make use of the expertise of a man who has done so much to help get the game to its present position.

D.B. Whitaker
Great Britain Olympic Coach 1984 and 1988

INTRODUCTION

This book is aimed at helping embryo coaches and players. It provides guidelines on how to structure and plan coaching messages to improve communication with pupils: in other words, how to coach well. This book is designed to help you construct a simple programme for coaching the game. It should guide you through the obstacles and provide an insight into what a good coach can achieve. You need not worry that you won't be able to follow a complex manual because this book isn't one, nor is it intended to be.

You might be a young teacher who is running a school team for the first time. The general principles apply but you may well find your task easier, in that some of the facilities will be at hand and more available. Whoever you are - parent, coach, player, teacher, a young student of P.E. or simply an interested sportsman, the characteristics of good coaching apply.

John Law

This book is dedicated to Mrs Olwen Law

AUTHOR'S ACKNOWLEDGEMENTS

The author would like to thank the following: David Whitaker, for all his help and advice; Mike Hamilton, for his assistance over the last five years; the National Coaching Foundation, for permission to reproduce parts of the Childrens Resource Pack; Simon Mason, for the original graphics and diagrams; Mark Smith, Alex Keating, Simon Mears, Philip Hardy, Chris Munton, and Craig Luker - photographic models for the artwork; Young Internationals Martin Langston and Paul McLean for their valuable suggestions; Richard Galbraith, the goalkeeping model; Janet Willis, for reading and processing.

THE AUTHOR

John Law was educated at Oxford University and started coaching hockey at Brune Park School, Gosport where one of the early stars was David Faulkner who is now an International player. In 1979 he moved to be Deputy Head of Saintbridge School, Gloucester, where several Under-18 and Under-21 International players were produced in three years. In 1982 he became Headmaster of Katharine Lady Berkeley's School in Gloucestershire where his coaching of the Under-11 group from local primary schools happened by accident when younger brothers asked him to join them. Now over twenty-five seven- to eleven-year-olds regularly attend his training sessions.

John Law is also Manager of the England Under-16 and Under-15 National teams, and is a member of the International Teams Committee of the Hockey Association. He is also Secretary, and a past Match Secretary of the English Schoolboys Hockey Association.

He has frequently taken young people of both sexes to Holland and Germany on hockey tours, and has given demonstrations at several coaching conferences.

He is particularly anxious in the near future to see greater coordination of youth hockey in clubs.

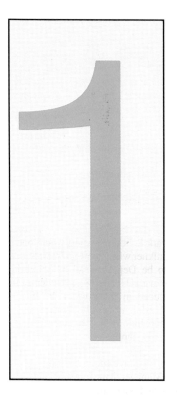

WHAT MAKES A GOOD COACH?

What Makes A Good Coach?

What makes a good coach? You need the normal human qualities of friendliness, honesty, enthusiasm and a competitive spirit. You should want to learn and improve your coaching to help others. You should act as a guide to the playing of the game, be receptive to ideas, answer questions readily and admit your mistakes. You should have plans and aims, some idea of how you are going to achieve them and believe in your ability to do so. Don't worry about whether other coaches are better or worse - they'll always be different.

You are the initiator, the first contact a beginner has with a wonderful game. Hockey is a technical and physical sport, potentially complex but at its best very simple, and how you introduce it is very important. How do you create the right atmosphere? At that critical first training session with beginners your priority should be to make them feel at ease. Convince them that you know what you are doing, that you are relaxed and they (like you) don't need to panic. The beginner needs to be reassured, to be active in learning as quickly as possible and to enjoy the game as soon as the stick is picked up.

The beginner also needs to know clearly what is expected of him in both realistic and clear terms. Coaches who aim low, achieve less. Beginners need their self-esteem and it's easy for the coach to put players off simply by not demanding enough. The coach is working well when demands are made on the beginner without him consciously realizing it. The beginner then regards whatever achievement he makes as his own idea.

Much has been written about motivation. Clubhouse discussions as to why certain coaches are good motivators usually, in my experience, put this down to good 'communication skills'. A lot of this is camouflage. Almost everyone communicates without conscious analysis - it's the desire to put the message across that counts. Be brave and remember that the beginner won't argue with you or dispute your authority if you've convinced him you know what you are talking about and your teaching has structure. This is called coaching!

Here are some vital coaching dos and don'ts:

DO
• Provide leadership by making decisions
• Be clear in your demands and use simple instructions
• Involve every player as soon as possible
• Encourage and promote self-esteem in the players by congratulation and praise
• Permit the unorthodox if it works
• Permit self expression
• Teach to your threshold of expectation
• Promote competition even against the clock
• Ask players to play to their maximum achievable level
• Above all MAKE IT FUN, MAKE THEM FEEL THEY ARE ACHIEVING.

DON'T
• Yell - too much
• Show you have particular hang-ups
• Permit unfair conduct. Never be afraid of encouraging players to beat their opponents: hockey is, after all, a competitive game
• Overpraise. You will deceive no one.

You should also be aware of what beginners want from a coaching session. They want:
• To enjoy, to learn and to win
• Fair treatment - and if they receive it, they are more likely to treat others fairly
• Security - they like to know where they stand with the coach
• Variety - so mix practices and types of work
• Simplicity in all things, explanations and practices
• To preserve self-esteem and like the coach to take a personal interest.

As a coach you also require certain things from your coaching:
• Fulfilment
• Enjoyment and fun
• Manifest signs of the effectiveness of your coaching
• Help.

Help is needed because very few coaches are able to predict the exact numbers, quality of players or the varying needs of individuals within a group. Ask for help from players to assist you in the coaching of individual skills, and from non-players, parents and friends who can make your life much easier by doing the jobs for which specific knowledge of hockey is not necessary. There are always people who would like to assist with things like booking facilities, arranging kit, helping with transport and a host of other vital administrative chore, so give them the opportunity. This help also gives you the time during sessions to analyze, reset a practice or set up new and different exercises.

Summary

Checklist for coaches:
• Be sunny, patient and positive
• Be organized and realistic
• Be fair and humorous
• Believe in yourself and your players.

Checklist for coaches involved with the young beginner:
• Work them within their limits
• Keep it Simple (KIS)
• Explain clearly, demonstrate accurately
• Insist they practise properly and correct faults individually
• Make sure you stress important points
• Make practices shorter the younger the player
• Play a game as soon as possible after introducing them to hockey, preferably at the end of the first session.

Avoid:
• Greater expectations than reasonable
• Jargon
• Negative feedback
• Complexity in language and practices.

PRACTICAL COACHING

Practical Coaching

Most coaches believe that working out a syllabus is the first task when organizing a coaching course, but your plans could well be conditioned by the facilities available. You would be well advised to assess first the resources available and the practical possibility of your plans.

The venue

It is tempting for the coach to want a full-size grass pitch but if you have access to a good one, you're lucky. In fact you do not need a pitch, you need a **smooth**, hard surface which can be indoors or outdoors and should be at least 36 feet by 18 feet, though you can probably manage with less by reducing the number of players. The numbers of course will determine what you need and for how long, but resist the temptation to pack any number into your facility.

Timing

Select the best time for your beginners and ensure the club supports you with necessary cash and secretarial skills. Notify each of your players of your arrangements by letter as this makes for good public relations and is generally more time-effective than phoning.

Equipment

Now you have selected the venue, check the equipment you need and ensure the club backs you. You would be well advised to start with your demands high but realistic.

Insist upon the correct kit and equipment for safety and legal reasons. You need sticks which are the right size, length and width. Avoid the use of 'junior' sticks which are considerably less than two inches wide at the bottom and generally make life more difficult for the learner and you!

Insist on one ball per player, especially if your pitch adjoins pasture. You will always need plenty of balls and losses/breakages will surprise the new coach. Mini-hockey balls weighing three and a half ounces are ideal for very young players.

KEY TO DIAGRAMS

Ball and ... path of ball

Player with the ball

Player without the ball

Shot at goal

Player in possession or in attacking team

Defender or opponent

Flag, cone or coaching aid

Stick head

Cones and bibs are a necessity, not a luxury. Don't forget the obvious like whistles and goal 'posts' if you're training on tennis courts.

Some clubs will shudder at your next request for a First Aid Kit and they'll positively buckle at the knees when you insist on a proper one, not a luncheon box full of plasters! Remember that **ice,** whether packed in a chemical pack or the genuine article, is vital. If you know of a parent who is a qualified First Aider, then that's a bonus.

A 'go-for', a right-hand person with a car in attendance is more than a luxury, and this person may well be your administrator. Simple things such as knowing the location of the nearest telephone should be remembered, as should Murphy's Law as what you think couldn't happen almost certainly will - so be prepared!

More is written about equipment in Chapter 6 but you are now ready to consider your programme.

Planning the Coaching Programme

Sessions should be structured. The generally-accepted view is that a warm-up/introduction takes about 15 minutes, the skill development practices 30 minutes, and the mini-game or competition the final 15 minutes, assuming a one hour session. You can squeeze more out of one hour on a pitch by introducing the warm-up concept off the pitch but nearby, before the booking time. A ten to 15 minute stretch and loosening exercise session not only saves time but creates the right atmosphere for work once upon the surface. You will find the players are eager to keep going.

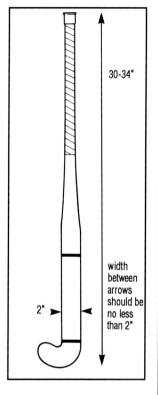

30-34"

width between arrows should be no less than 2"

2"

The ideal junior hockey stick

The 'three-phase' session breaks down as follows:
1. **The warm-up and introduction**
2. **Skill and development**
3. **The game.**

1. The warm-up and introduction

This phase is vital. Never omit it, and insist it becomes automatic for the players before any activity. The warm-up can vary in content but generally includes jogging - though never running at anywhere near full pace, stretching and loosening the joints. Make sure that stretching is useful, so when stretching a particular muscle, insist that players hold the stretch for 20 to 30 seconds otherwise the value is lost. You can split the warm-up into group and individual exercises. You can often find a leader by finding someone to take these exercises. If you feel you need help here consult a Physical Education teacher at a local school, who will know what is required.

If you are warming up off the pitch then what you do will be constrained, but on the pitch the warm-up continues with ball and stick exercises, which vary according to the session. For a pre-match session, penalty corners and so forth should be practised but for training, groups of three or four practising simple skills such as hitting, pushing and receiving in five to six yard squares are good sample exercises.

Do not forget your goalkeepers. If they are to be in at the beginning they need to be warmed up, and this is where you can use a senior player to help, while you supervise the rest. Remember that warming up a goalkeeper means feeding balls to each leg and hand, and not blasting a ball into the roof of the net. Here your surplus balls are most useful. A handy tip with group practices is to advise players to have a spare ball nearby so that in the event of a missed control, valuable time is not wasted in retrieval.

2. Skill and development

1. Demonstrating a skill needs careful handling. Always insist on the attention of everyone and do not permit individuals to fiddle with a ball while you are showing a skill - they won't learn and the others are distracted.

It is not cheating to select the optimum part of the pitch and the best player - whether on the coaching team, or within the group - to help your demonstration. Use an experienced, skilled player to Indian dribble, for example, and simply ask him to freeze in a position you want to emphasize. If the demonstration goes wrong don't panic; remember the group can't do it either! There is an old adage that if your first demonstration is perfect you should leave it at that because the next one is never as good. Simply use all your resources to get the message across.

2. The next phase will often throw the new coach. After the demonstration everyone is keen to try for themselves. Before you let them experiment, insist on **discipline and direction** because if they don't all travel in the same direction collisions will occur. New players, especially, find it difficult to keep their head and eyes up, so you can use a collision to your advantage! Stop the practice with a whistle (short and loud) and point (heartlessly!) to the two unfortunates rubbing their heads to demonstrate what happens if a player does not frequently look up, and why you are right to demand that everyone moves in the same general direction.

3. Now you should encourage **individual** corrections of a fault, and the timing here is crucial. Give them time to learn and practise but then get them into partner situations to introduce the element of pressure. For example, you can create a mini-race in pairs or arrange that two players run at each other on command and dribble to miss each other, see illustration below.

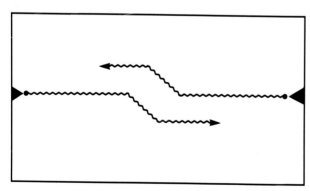

The 'run at each other'
practice

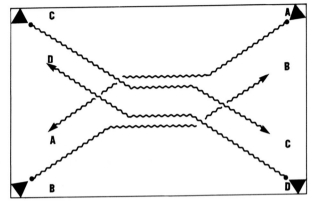

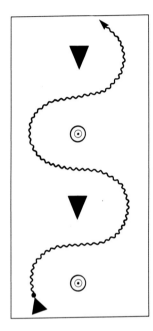

Top right: Royal Tournament practice
Above: Slalom dribble

4. You can now move on to **practices** with groups of fours or sixes (don't forget to count your players at the beginning). In this particular skill there are many variations. A favourite of mine is to create a square of ten metres and have players at each corner, two dribbling across the diagonal to opposite points. This encourages skill, pace and keeping the eyes up. Later all four players can go together, rather like the motor cyclists in the Royal Tournament. It's good fun and you can call the practice by some nickname, like the 'motor-cyclists'. Next time, all you need to do is say 'motor-cyclists' and they will set it up themselves.

Throughout these exercises you have been encouraging and supporting individuals while they are doing this. Don't stand in one place like a bandmaster - go round each group. Keep the theme simple (you've already set your target). Your groups will be showing variations in attainment and you can now become devious.

5. Change some individuals in the groups so you reduce the mixed attainment situation, particularly if there are two excellent and two poor in one quartet, as the top two become very frustrated if they can't progress quicker.

When you reset your groups you can do it without damning the less able. Go to a good group and suggest quietly that they might develop the practice. A refinement of my example could be as they run across the diagonal to ask them to exchange balls, a remarkably difficult little skill incorporating all sorts of talents, particularly footwork. You will, of course, have written down your practices. I prefer to use postcards, which can be shuffled as used. Don't be reluctant to let your groups see you revising the practices; they should know by now that you are organized - and of course you are, growing in confidence every session.

Develop your range of exercises and skill as a coach by asking players to enhance basic exercises. This can consist of:
• Increased accuracy
• Increased skill
• Increased complexity
• Skills performed under pressure (from opponents)
• Skills performed in tight situations, smaller areas.

So, for example, when developing the Indian dribble skill, demand more accuracy and control with balance, good footwork and a little more speed. Ask then for a dribble on an 'S'-shaped run. Put in cones and/or players to tackle so that a new dimension is introduced. Then reduce the space or put cones closer together to 'tighten' the practice.

I've used this only to show how a simple skill can be developed, and you'll be amazed how the time has flown while this is going on. You can develop all your basics, as you will see in more detail in later chapters.

3. The game

The last part of our three-phase session is the game. Here the coach's experience is vital. Don't just assemble some players (in multi colours!) and play.

Make the game a variation of a skill. Use small teams of four, five or six-a-side depending on the area, make sure the game is properly umpired within sensible parameters, and that each team is similarly dressed. Youngsters are vexed by confusion which leads to insecurity. If they can't identify their team mates when playing the game and if they can't see **consistency** in the umpiring, then you could have a revolt on your hands. If you decide to ignore the rule relating to the contact between foot and ball, **be consistent** about it. Never tolerate obstruction or serious stick-bashing, however, as these habits should be stopped at the beginning. Fussy penalizing of 'feet' and 'ball off the body' are sure ways of slowing up and spoiling the game. To begin with just let them play.

Relate your game to the skill. In Chapter 5 we will look at conditioned games, but you can set up simple request games where you ask for a skill to be emphasized. You can usually raise a laugh by penalizing a 'bad' piece of play for incompetence. Youngsters would rather be penalized for that than for infringing the rules.

In encouraging the Indian dribble, for example, you could employ a 'no-tackling outside the circle' rule. Experiment with your own ideas but convince them that you have worked it out.

At the end of the session, get the players to clear up and insist on a ball count or you might regret it next week!

Try to do a brief evaluation with and, later, without the players. Remember to evaluate in simple terms what you've done and note what you will need to revise next week. There should always be an overlap of activity.

Coaching Without Stick and Ball

At higher levels, much work can be done by athletics' coaches to improve hockey players' footwork. Although, of course, lots of work to encourage this can be worked on in a normal session, this section is devoted to sedentary skills.

Now that video is commonplace, it performs a useful function, along with other visual material, in the coaching programme. It is very important, however, that it is used wisely.

Avoid the extremes of running through a three-hour programme without any comment or with frequent interruptions.

Select a goal-ridden game and show, say, the first half almost without interruption, and then ask your players for a general impression of the game. Focus minds on the next half and what to look for. In this way you can avoid having to stop the video, and can simply talk briefly over the commentary. For excitement choose a video with commentary, though you may cringe at some of the words of wisdom. To young people, the background noise seems critical. You can later use clips of the video to demonstrate a point, and obviously it is better if you've run through the video yourself, in advance. Whatever you do, do not let the session become one-paced or run it without a break.

There are now high-quality coaching videos which have taken excellent filmclips of good hockey practice and put them in a teaching context. Coaches are strongly urged to use these videos since they supplement the basic coaching programme. They are easier to use than the home video of a game, especially the unedited versions. The condensed videos of particular tournaments are also excellent, and very useful for introducing the game at a parents' evening in the clubhouse.

The following three-stage development plan will help you to explain to parents and club members what you are doing in the short, medium, and long-term.

Note
In the early stages it is an excellent idea to appoint a Match Manager who referees from the middle of the pitch and coaches **both or neither side**. Coaches should stay off the pitch during games and say as little as possible.

A Simple Three-Stage Development Plan For Young People Seven To Twelve Years			
	Coaching notes	Suggested playing surface	Umpiring notes
Stage one (Up to eight years)	• Coach elementary skills with emphasis on safety. • Play small team games.	• Use flat pitches- tarmac, synthetic or good dry grass.	• Basic rules only, mostly to eliminate dangerous play. • Match manager only.
Stage two (Eight to eleven years)	• Train on full-size pitch • Play matches on 1/4 size pitch, progressing from five- to six- and eight-a-side.	• Use flat pitches - as above.	• Rules as for mini-hockey. Emphasis on eliminating dangerous play. • Match manage.
Stage three (Eleven to thirteen years)	• Train on 1/2 size pitch. • Play matches on 1/4 to full size	• Use flat pitches including reasonable to good grass and shale.	• Official rules. • For substitutions, however, use ice hockey rules.

You may, of course, have someone who can video a coaching session (incidentally, it is not worth doing unless the action can be filmed from a high vantage-point). By all means use this facility but be careful not to destroy the image and ego of a player which, unfortunately, is easily done on video. Be as supportive as you can during your critical analysis of personal skills.

Some coaches also use diaries for players to record their training and to help arrange visits to good league matches and Internationals - both of which are important for player imitation, general hero-worship and autographs. You may be able to programme this in by playing a game near the venue and watching the match afterwards to make a day out.

Summary

Checklist for practical coaching
1. Book the facility. Personnel available.
2. Check kit and equipment.
3. Plan the content of the warm-up.
4. Work from notes for the skill part of the session and its development. Set targets.
5. Decide on the game, the number of players to be involved, the conditions and aims.
6. Evaluate. Make a revision plan for next session.

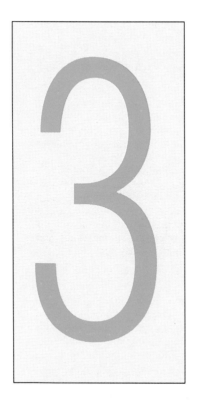

COACHING THE INDIVIDUAL SKILLS

Coaching the Individual Skills

Remember to use and check your aids, and be flexible in taking advantage of the lines and boxes marked for badminton and tennis on tarmac and sports-hall floors.

You may need to set up a grid, which generally needs to be ten metres square and can be easily converted into an extended grid ten metres by twenty. Much can be done using the basic grid.

The Grip

It is essential to coach this properly even if you run the risk of appearing fussy. A correct grip is the key to good play: dribbling, tackling and all methods of beating the opponent. With the correct grip, the player can **'make the ball strong'** to the right and in front of the player , which is the strongest position to take the ball forward and transfer it rapidly to a team-mate. It is the single skill on which many others in the game depend and without which a player has a very limited future, so it's worth spending time and energy on getting it right.

A simple way of teaching the basic grip is to lay the stick down with the face flat on the floor, and ask the players to pick it up at the top with the left hand. Ensure that the hand is not twisted in any way, and then instruct them to add the right hand at a comfortable position down the stick, but not too far down. Emphasize that the left hand grips and twists the stick, rotating through to the right. The right wrist does **not** rotate. This is a common early fault and should not be allowed. Stress that whatever happens, the left hand is always to the left of the right hand, even when the ball is outside the left foot, to avoid the cross-over of hands on the stick.

Follow this by placing the ball in front of the left foot and simply move it across the body from the left to the right and back, stressing that the ball must not come back towards the feet, at present. It is useful to insist on the nose following the ball as this

The basic grip

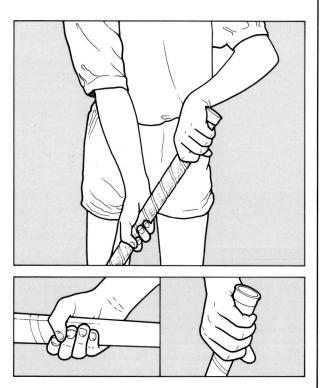

makes the eyes follow and the shoulders sway, a useful attribute which is discussed later. If the twist of the stick is not correct, the ball will drift back under the body, and this will be penalized. Later this movement, together with good footwork, can be used to beat a player, but for the time being concentrate on the hand and stick skill.

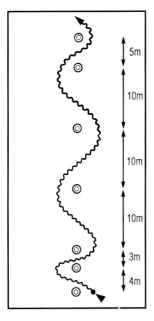

5m

10m

10m

10m

3m

4m

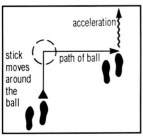

acceleration

stick
moves
around
the
ball

path of ball

Top: Slalom dribble practice
Above: Over-the-top dummy

Beating a Man

Developing this skill is relatively easy as young players always want to beat a man and you can now oblige them! From the simple left-to-right movement, change to a walk using the same skill so the ball is moving in a zigzag fashion.

When this is accomplished, get the players to perform this skill at a gentle run, emphasizing that **missing the ball** (which will happen) **does not matter**. Check individually the hand positions of your players. Encourage them to run in as straight a line as possible and, even at this stage, try to ensure that heads and eyes are up to retain all-round vision. A good practice for this skill is the slalom, using cones at varying distances according to the skill level achieved.

Now that the dribble has been established from the grip, it is possible to teach a 'dummy'. New players will like this as it is an obvious achievement. The 'over-the-top-dummy' is simple. The ball is moved in front of the body and the stick describes a semicircle over it without making contact, while the body-weight and shoulders dip to the left. The ball is then moved square, left-to-right, and after about one metre 'straightened' into a forward motion. The coach should now emphasize the need for quick acceleration to take the player past the defender who, 'buying' the dummy, has shifted to the right, giving the player his reverse stick or difficult side to run through. Stress that **pace and acceleration** are the keys to this skill.

Try to put the whole thing together in a **smooth** movement, checking that the footwork is so nimble that the skill comes easily. Most youngsters pick this up in a few minutes.

Usually, the Indian dribble and this dummy are adequate to show the importance of the grip, and you can now look at more ways of beating a player in one-versus-one situations.

The contact dribble, which includes the skill of keeping the ball on the end of the stick when running at full speed, is a fundamental skill. The secret is to run, in early practices, at a jogging speed with the ball as far in front as possible, to the right of the line of running. Stress the need to keep the eyes up and looking for the next movement. In further practices the speed can be varied, as

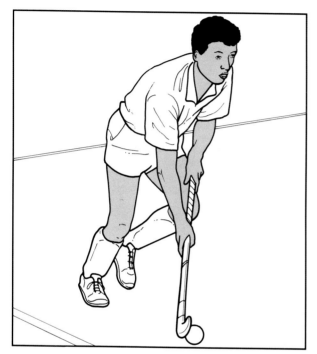

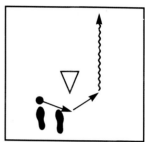

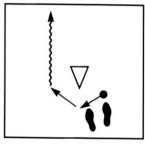

Above left: The perfect carrying and contact dribble body position
Top: Left-to-right pattern
Above: Right-to-left pattern

can the skill of changing the pace.

Next, you can ask them to run in an 'S' manner, trying to keep the ball 'strong' on the open, right-hand side. In a slalom practice the ball is likely to move left off the stick as the player moves left, and this is the most common problem. You need here to emphasize footwork and body movement. Both must be geared to move around the back of the ball as it travels left, to get back into the 'strong' position. Again, eyes should be up.

Once this fundamental skill is reasonably performed, you are able to add several methods of beating a man, which all involve running with the ball as described, good footwork and the use of disguise, all performed with the 'eyes up' for as long as possible.

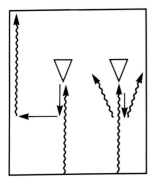

Check and box dummy

Practices to Establish Good Ball Skill

1. With the ball in front of the right foot, move it backwards to the left a metre, about 45° behind square. Straighten up and then dribble (contact or Indian). Footwork is essential; try to get the players' feet working with the stick and the ball.
2. The ball on left-hand side is moved backwards at 45° to the right, then forwards at 45°, then straight ahead. Again, footwork is crucial.

Several other patterns can be worked on, but almost all involve moving the ball backwards to take it away from a tackle or an oncoming player. The footwork has to be light, 'ballet'-like, and the feet should move in **harmony** with the stick and ball, as David Whitaker (GB player and Director of Coaching) puts it.

The most important of these patterns is the left-to-right transfer of the ball followed by the swivel of the body across so that the ball is in a strong, almost unassailable position.

The open-side dummy is a basic skill but difficult to achieve instantly. The 'contact' position is used and the dummy is a swivel of body and shoulders to the right, with the stick behind the ball to fake a pass to the right. The body-swerve throws the defender on to his reverse side, opening the 'easy' or open side of the defender for the attacker to move the ball quickly to the left, probably between 30 ° and 50 ° from square. The ball can then be quickly made 'strong' on the open side, using pace to accelerate past the defender who has been wrong-footed by the dummy. There **must** be a dummy... you will find that players often forget the faked pass, fail to throw the defender , and just drift left down the easy side of the defender who is balanced and in a good tackling position. Watch carefully for this and eliminate the problem at an early stage. Build up to this skill by practising at a jogging pace first and gradually quickening. The whole action must be smoothly done and well-practised.

The last of these dummies suitable for coaching at this stage is the 'check' or 'check and box' dummy - my terminology.

With the ball, again, in a strong contact-dribble position, the player moves to the side running with the left shoulder leading. (The ability to run sideways is important and should be included in warm-up to remind players!). He 'shows' the ball to the defender, inducing the opponent to lean forward and lose balance. The ball is stopped and then moved backwards- say, two metres - and then moved forward past the defender who is still committed, off-balance. The 'box' dummy is similar but the ball is moved square left after the 'check' and then forward, forming a sort of 'box'.

The basic principles of all these are **smooth running**, excellent **footwork** and as much **acceleration** as possible. Add clever **disguise** by the body and shoulders and you have a checklist for these skills. Youngsters like these skills and you can, in my opinion, afford to be indulgent because they will overdo them in games. Be patient. Remember that a very skilled player can always be taught to play in a team. What you can't do is expect a player with no skill to beat a man and this is obviously a severe limitation. In Europe, all players have to be able to beat a man, even - and especially - sweepers!

Propelling the Ball

You may notice the absence of the usual 'push' or 'hit' words. Now on artificial grass or hard surfaces, it's possible to 'slap' a ball hard with hands apart, a style the 'old' coach would never permit.

Hitting is hit and miss! Pushing the ball for , say, an Under-10 is difficult. It is not moving the ball which is hard, but putting pace on it. The effect of this on a game is to cause bunching of players since the ball is always in a confined space. Therefore it is vital for players to establish ball speed as soon as possible, and you needn't be too worried as to how this is achieved.

There are, however, some important technical points to note to help youngsters develop the 'slap' into a 'push' and 'hit'. The first problem is that up to this stage the ball has been in front of the body and 'sideways' movements have rarely been used. Now

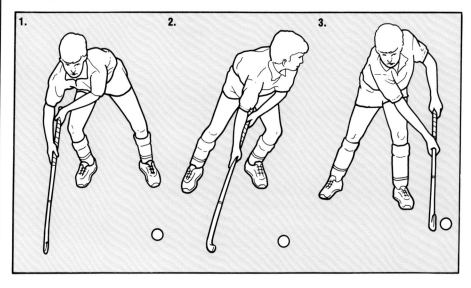

1.   2.   3.

The 'slap' or push-hit
The body weight moves onto the left knee to receive the ball (1). The weight then moves across the knees from right to left (2) to finish in position (3) after 'contact'.

you'll have to stress that power (which creates ball speed) moves down the line of knee and shoulder so 'sideways' stance and foot position are critical, as they are for pushing, hitting and aerial play. So when teaching any sort of slap, push or hit, insist on proper foot and shoulder position, or all your work will go to waste. Slapping a ball means a 'push-hit' with hands apart and quite a lot of bottom hand. The sideways body stance resembles cricket and is not a natural position (ask a cricket coach) and so always has to be taught. If not trouble will ensue.

You can easily move on from allowing the 'slap' to become a genuine push with the stick and ball permanently in contact. This may, however, expose bad coaching of the slap since the knee/shoulder weight transfer from right foot to the left foot is so critical that poor technique will mean no ball speed. The stick will describe an arc as the body 'twists' and the ball goes off at all angles. My first attempt at coaching this led to several bruises and a broken window! Use some means of stressing that everything literally goes down the line of the ball, including the follow-through.

Practices here are important because you want to encourage the automatic nature of the skill. Don't use complex practices as they're not necessary. Pairs, spaced ten metres apart, can practise quite adequately. Do not give a lot of individual help, and vary the distances and the tempo of the practice.

The next natural progression is 'slapping' or pushing a moving ball. Stress here the need for nimble footwork, because at the point of propulsion the power generated by the side-on position and weight transfer is still vital. In simple terms the concept is one of over-taking the ball, changing to a 'side-on' position and, during the backlift, allowing the ball to come level with the left foot, at which point the ball is actually slapped or pushed by the stick.

In the various practices illustrated here, you will derive a bonus from starting on the 'reverse-side'. The ball will at some time, inevitably be sliced on to the partner's left foot or outside, and the player already knows how to retrieve it and get it into the 'strong' or push-slap position. At this point mention ice-hockey where the 'slap' certainly propels the puck and at some pace. The Canadians usually have some good ice-hockey players in their National 'Field' Hockey Teams.

This skill, coupled with the next, can be boring in practice, so try to vary your programme, particularly in grids, where you can go from a ten-metre propulsion to the twenty-metre, which is one-third of the pitch width.

From a static push position, angle the practice so a player has to rotate to make several pushes side-on. Practices are quite easy to develop but stress the footwork. In Chapter 8, we deal with more reverse stick work and pushing off the 'wrong', right foot! The principles are still the same.

A good push position

Checklist
- Footwork and weight transfer
- Eyes on the ball
- Right hand power
- Ball position is correct
- Grip. Left hand slightly further round to leading edge.

Controlling the Ball

Controlling the ball from the left
The ball is controlled outside the right shoulder (1) before being moved forward at 90° from the pass.

The player takes the ball early (2) because the ball is going back where it came from.

You will notice that we're not stopping the ball, a skill which is now rarely desirable except at short corners (see Chapter 7). The common factor, whether controlling a ball from left, right, front or behind, is that the players must learn to keep the next move in mind. Control, look, act is not as good as **look, control, act**.

• From the left

The target control area is the right shoulder, certainly to the right of the left foot. If the player is going to move left with the ball, then the control is nearer to the left foot and if passing, or moving to the right, then further to the right, even outside the right shoulder. Lining up the eye and stick is important and, having decided what to do next, a careful eye on the ball is essential.

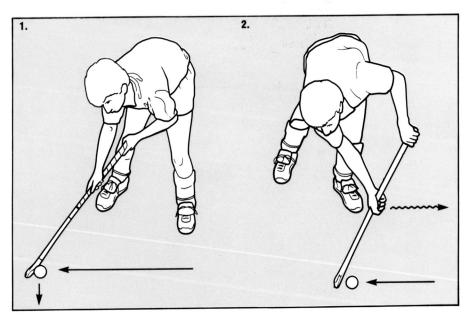

1.

2.

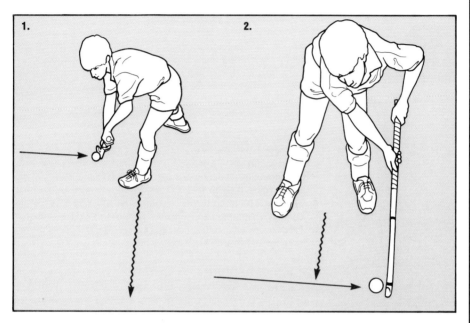

• From the right

The ball is controlled either before it arrives at the right shoulder on the open side, with eyes and body leaning over, to prevent the ball popping up. Taken at pace, the ball is in the strong position which makes life difficult for a defender.

Alternatively, the player can take the ball outside the left shoulder, having allowed it to pass across the body. This requires a footwork adjustment in running with the ball, and one-handed skills are often useful after the control. Alternatively the ball has to be moved from left to right into the strong position.

Of course the players can employ the shoulder swerve taught at the beginning to 'dummy' the control. In each of the above cases, they should pretend to take the ball early and then follow it across the body without touching it until the last possible moment and accelerate away. This nuance needs to be practised with a defender 'buying' the body swerve initially.

Controlling the ball from the right
The ball from the right is controlled, open side (1).
The ball from the right passes across the body (2) and will then need to be moved forward.

33

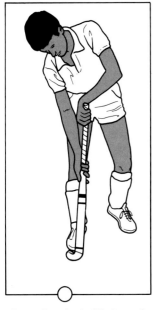

Controlling the ball in front of right foot

One of the best practices for ball control is remarkably simple. Use a 20 metres by ten rectangle (the extended grid), with four players pushing or slapping two balls from opposite corners along the outside lines to each other. The balls can be passed either to the left, in an anti-clockwise direction, or in a clockwise direction. Either way the use of the feet is crucial. You can vary this by using two players and dribbling with a push and control. This practises all the skills mentioned so far.

• From the front

This requires an upright stick, controlling between the line of the feet facing the ball. One also needs to be able to control the ball in front or slightly to the left of the left foot, as well as in front or to the right of the right foot, but this latter situation is natural and easy. It helps to stress that the body weight is slightly forward to produce an alert position. Some players point the stick at the ball as it comes toward the control to line it up.

• From behind

This requires the greatest skill and coordination. Timing is helped by eye contact and that particular skill is fully discussed later. What must be said simply before demonstration, is that obstruction is the problem. The player has to show where the ball is to come either to the right or left as he runs down the line of the ball towards its origin. Either way the trick is to get the ball strong by turning clockwise and pulling the ball back away from any defender. A static practice here is of little use, since movement is critical if the ball is to be taken away from the tackler. Be static in a game and you'll soon be aware of a defender hammering at your back door! Therefore practise this as a moving skill, using both reverse stick and open side followed by footwork. You can also introduce the notion of showing a blade to indicate where the player wants the ball. This reinforces the idea look (then show the blade), control and act (usually by running or passing).

The bottom line is, of course, that the ball has to be moved into the strong position from wherever it's received as **quickly** and smoothly as possible. Do not coach this on a bumpy pitch as it will simply demolish your previous confidence-building work! Practices here are legion but do vary them and try to build up the stress situation which is the rogue factor in control. This practice is so easy in a no-stress situation and so unreal! Use active defenders after passive ones (for example), smaller space and varying angles. Organize practices in fours with three players putting the fourth player under a variety of pressures.

• On the reverse or difficult side of the stick

This is relatively easy to explain, more difficult to do and even more taxing to perform at a very high standard. It's a skill particularly handy for left-handed players and if you find one, look after this player because left halves and defenders are precious!

When the ball comes to the left foot, or outside, encourage the player to control it with the stick on the open side. If this is not possible because the ball is travelling too fast and wide of the left foot, then two possibilities arise. Firstly, a simple stop on the reverse side using both hands(as described in the section on basic grip) can be used or, alternatively, a stop made the stick flat on the ground, as used in indoor hockey. The control can be one-handed for balls at a distance, with the stick angled forward at about 45° to avoid the ball going under the crook. This has the disadvantage in that the player will be in a low position and it takes a little more

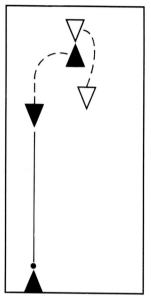

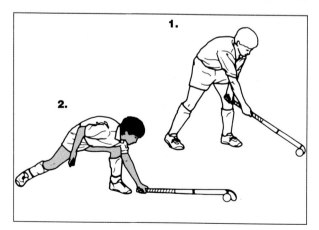

Above: Controlling the ball from behind, the attacker turns off his defender and collects the moving ball.
Left: Controlling the ball on the reverse side; two-handed (1) and one-handed (2) for distance.

Checklist
Body position breaks down into:
• Position of eyes
• Footwork
• Arms and stick.
And, of course, this should be geared to where the player wants to play the ball after the control.

time to get the ball into the strong position by the right foot and also, if tackled in this position, the opponent, upright and with both hands on the stick, will be able to force the ball through the flat stick.

It is important to move the ball as quickly as possible into the strong position ready to perform the next skill. Players must be able to execute both skills, since the ball will inevitably come on to the difficult reverse side whether intended or not, though open-sided skills should always be encouraged.

In simple terms a player has to be able to deal with the ball in all positions, including any lifted ball, though that particular skill is detailed in the later section on aerial work.

Hitting and Shooting

This is one of the most difficult skills for a beginner to master and one of the most frustrating for a coach. In the past a great deal was made of technique, but you will inevitably find some players who are natural hitters and others whose hitting needs to be manufactured. It is always time-saving to teach hitting in conjunction with shooting and it also gives the player satisfaction when the ball rips into the net at great speed. Your ability as a coach is tested since within any group the achievement rate will vary enormously.

One can start with a static, fairly regimented practice so as to minimize danger which should always be an important consideration. Using both goals, organize a semi-circle of hitters and employ the goalkeepers after a while. First however, you'll need to do a simple demonstration to help those whose skills will need to be 'manufactured'. Stress the following:

• Sideways position, ball opposite the front foot and nose over it with the left shoulder leading. Try to prevent the front foot from twisting during the hit, or balance and power will be lost.

• Hands should be together with no gap between them, and not overlapping as in golf. The 'V' between thumb and forefinger should line up with the leading edge of the stick.

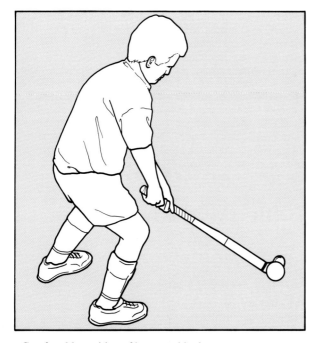

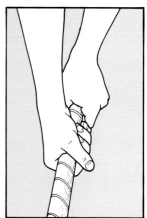

Hitting
Left: The perfect position
Below: The correct grip

• Comfortable position of knees and body.
• Check that there is a reasonable but not great backlift and a good swing. Some players will chop down on the ball as if using an axe, and some will change body position during the hit which results in an 'air' shot or complete miss!

Do emphasize, as a coach, the importance of finding the natural way, and not worrying about style too much. Also, ask the player to hit the ball towards the goal and do not worry too much about pace.

The follow-through is as important in hockey as it is in cricket and golf, and you will soon spot those who have played those games. If the follow-through goes down the line of the ball, you'll prevent foot twist and ensure an accurate hit.

Encouragement, particularly with youngsters, is vital. There is also the trick of asking a youngster with a big stick to drop both

Checklist of faults in hitting and shooting:
- Awkward body position
- Eyes not on the ball at the time of striking
- Poor bottom hand
- High elbow
- Rigidity of movement: emphasize the smooth flow of hit
- Transference of body weight from right to left as in the slap and push
- Foot-twist and follow-through which should be limited in height.

hands down the stick to hit a ball Asian-style. Best results are, strangely, had on grass, since there is give for a slight mis-hit. A rigid surface is unforgiving!

The next stage is hitting a moving ball. Again, you can use a simple shooting practice but it is sensible to employ a simple hitting practice against a wall so as to get a return ball. Make sure everyone has at least one ball each, as there's nothing worse than waiting to hit. The essentials are few in number but often fun to watch. The basics are as for the hitting of a stationary ball, because if one used a 'freeze frame', the position of a player hitting a moving ball would be the same: sideways on, head over, good backlift and follow-through. All you need to do is stress the **need to overtake the ball** so that the ball approaches the front foot during the backlift, so that **when the stick 'arrives', the ball is opposite the front foot.**

Practices are easy to develop - a simple roll of the ball, follow-up, and shoot. Try this from left to right. The body position is critical. Introduce the dummy and shot, dribble and shot, but above all, make it fun. Have a competition. Even without goalkeepers you'll be amazed at the miss rate but don't be downhearted. Remember how many open goals you have missed while playing the game.

Spend a lot of time on individuals, as these are personal skills.Later, you'll be able to develop hitting in any position, from the back foot for example, but it's easy if these basics are correct. You'll also need to introduce hitting under pressure from defenders, and this is when it gets really interesting. You can, of course, introduce a goalkeeper in these practices - you'll get a new angle on the meaning of low-scoring!

Individual practice is vital to this skill, no-one else can do it for the player. The more often the hit is practised, the better the achievement.

Tackling and Closing Down (or When Not to Tackle)

Soccer coaches stress that the dive into a tackle is almost always disastrous, and often hilarious! The same applies in hockey. Tackling is a limited skill - limited by the size of the player, movement, arm length and stick size. So the secrets of tackling are:
• When to tackle
• When not to tackle (called closing down)
• How to tackle.

When to tackle

This is simple to describe, but it's more difficult to stop players from following their suicidal instincts. In simple terms, one tackles when there is a good chance of obtaining possession, bearing in mind various factors, including the surface being played on. Players should try and judge how fast the attacker is, how skilful he is and, bearing in mind their position on the pitch, assess whether there is any need to tackle.

When not to tackle (closing down)

Instruct your pupils never to tackle when they have little chance of gaining possession. If an attempt is made and the ball is not gained, the player could well be on the wrong side of the attacker and effectively be temporarily out of the game. It could well be worthwhile for the coach to demonstrate this.

Youngsters like tackling as they win the ball and achieve obvious success. You'll have to put a rein on their instincts and this is where your skill as a good coach comes into play. The message here must be clear and simple - never tackle unless you have a good chance of success or you are desperate because a certain goal is the only other result.

Closing down is the skill of manoeuvring a player into a

position where a tackle is possible. This requires the following:
• Balance and nimble footwork
• Standing on the side you do not wish the player to travel so making him go the other way, usually on your open or strong side.

The idea is to slow down the opponent, limiting the space into which he can travel or pass the ball, to force him into error which gives the defender a better chance to tackle successfully. Tell the other players that they will also benefit because by slowing down the man with the ball, the whole defence has an easier job taking up marking and covering positions. This will be discussed later.

Make sure everyone can close down. If your attackers can close down the defenders, the ball stays in their half. A good team consists of eleven attackers who can defend.

How to tackle

There are three main types of tackle: the jab, open-side (block) tackle, and the reverse-stick tackle. There are some basics which apply to all three:
• Keep eyes on the ball
• Avoid distractions like dummies
• Be active, never stand back on your heels
• Pressurize or distract the attacker with movements of the stick and feet.

Jab tackle

Of the three types of tackle, the jab tackle is becoming more and more popular, particularly on hard surfaces, as it has an element of surprise. Use a demonstrator to extend his left leg and then with stick held only in the left hand, stretch out as far as possible. They'll be amazed at the tackling distance they can achieve from the rear foot: up to four to five metres. (That's why in teaching players to beat a man you must insist that the dummy or movement is at least four metres from a well-balanced defender.) The surprise element of the jab is that it comes in quickly, rather like a snake sticking out its tongue - fast and lethal! By the way, it helps with youngsters to use fantasy words. Why not use, as I do, the concept of stealing the ball from the opponent. A ferret also figures largely in my coaching vocabulary!

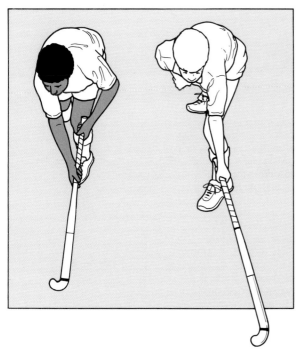

Jab tackle
The correct position for the one-handed and two-handed tackle. Note the angle of the stick and the way in which it protects the feet in the two-handed tackle.

The stick is angled at 45° as in the diagram above. This effectively blocks off the left-right movement of the attacker. The right hand can help, but essentially this is a one-handed skill so do not yell 'Get both hands on the stick' because. if they do, you'll halve their tackling radius. The secret of the jab is the sheer length of the tackle and its easy transfer into other tackles. Very occasionally two hands are better, especially when the defender is in his own circle and needs to protect his feet from the ball in case he gives away a short corner. The body is **sideways** on, **left shoulder leading**, but the player should be able to move quickly in other directions if necessary. Check that the tackler is not flat-footed and front-on. Try to encourage the jab which is never intended to get the ball, but is a feint to put the attacker off! It's amazing how often this works. The sudden dart of the stick into the attacker's vision often induces him to part with the ball - charitably!

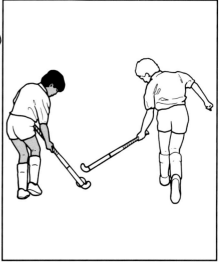

Above left: Two-handed reverse stick tackle
Above right: Preparing for the block tackle

Open side tackle

This is sometimes called a block tackle and is very effective - providing the player has been persuaded into a position to perform the tackle. The left foot is usually in the lead. This tackle is also done 'on the run', keeping the attacker as 'wide' as possible.

Reverse stick tackle

This is the most difficult both to teach and to perform. You can't touch the stick or body of an opponent so this has a high-skill tariff. To be successful the player should:
• **Always** get in a position to the **goal side** of attacker
• Trap the ball using reverse stick as strongly as possible
• Lock the left elbow for power.
Tackling can also be 'horizontal' but this can be dangerous because, if you make a mistake, recovery is slow or impossible. This tackle is good indoors where the rules prevent a lifted ball over the stick.

Tackling practices

Tackling practices are best done gently at first to stress success, so get the attacker to do predictable things such as running in a straight line. You can develop the practice by asking attackers to dummy, feint, or change direction.

One tip is to get an attacker to approach the defender on the side on which the defender is least confident. **Practise most what you need most.**

Coaching here is best done in 'pairs'. Analyze the skill in pairs and keep players active and interested by changing over the attacker/defender roles and use a confined space. Start using an area ten to fifteen metres by five metres wide with the defender in a central position and then limit the space, say, to five by five metres. Give the attacker a target like reaching the other end of the oblong, or opposite side of a square.

Forehand practices are better done with players initially running alongside the attacker. Later you can get the defender to force the attacker to the open side for a block tackle (sometimes called shadowing). In a block tackle stress the power of the left hand but also the idea of 'ferreting' the ball, especially on a hard surface where winning possession depends on the timing of the tackle.

These practices can be developed by using two or three defenders in line, with attackers getting a shot in only after they've got past these tacklers. This improves the skills of all, both defenders and attackers. Now stress the need for cooperation between tacklers. If the first tackler closes down, does the job of the second become easier?

Next, use three attackers (or four) versus two defenders and a goalkeeper with only one ball, say, in a 25-metre wide by 20-metre long box. Again you can revise the dribbling skills as well as coaching the tackle.

Here the good coach should deliberately mix in the use of other skills. This is vital not only for a sensible practice but also for individual tuition on the tackle itself.

Good coaches usually revise skills already learnt when introducing a new skill, as this saves time and is relevant to the game situation.

The Aerial Ball

Do not be frightened by this skill. Be assured that while it is not easy to coach, the beginner actually enjoys throwing the ball in the air once he knows how. When played into the air, the ball can be classified as one of three types, at this level: the flick or medium length aerial pass; the little lifted pass over the flat stick say about half a metre to one metre high; and the shot undercut into the upper part of the goal.

Coach the skill by describing it as a push made with the opened face of stick, in which the body is kept low, and ball in front of the left foot. Good weight transfer is essential, and again you might get better results on a grass or soft surface, since it's easier

Aerial ball
Early preparation for lifting the ball

then to put the stick under the ball. A simple practice is to play in pairs, five metres apart, one player lifting the ball into the hands of another. Always have a target even if it is only a painted line on a wall.

Obviously the good player can lift an aerial pass a good third of a pitch in length, some 30 metres, but for the little lifted pass over a defender's stick, more of a feel for the pass is desirable. With more and more hockey being played on artificial surfaces the little lifted ball is becoming a basic rather than an advanced skill. I recently saw a nine-year-old German boy use it over twenty times in one game to devastating effect. At this level we are coaching the simple ball played off the front foot but you will see better players, particularly in Germany, lift the ball from almost any body position - and if it works don't discourage it.

The third type of aerial ball is the lifted hit, sometimes called an undercut. Bearing in mind the danger aspect, the coaching of this skill can be very frustrating. When learning the hit, players will lift the ball accidentally but you will need to organize the technique.

The first requirement is to hit the ball slightly in front of the line of the left foot, so that the stick, on the hit, is beginning to rise - so lifting the ball. The position of the bottom or right hand is essential in this, as is the need for patience. I tend to emphasize the need to stand tall and 'climb through the ball', but each coach needs to develop his own patter as well as give a great deal of individual tuition.

You will need to coach the control of an aerial pass. I usually employ the concept of a frying pan in a pancake race. The aim is to point the stick head at the ball and take the 'way' or direction off the ball, putting the ball on the ground in the strong position in front of the body in order to do something with it. Discourage flail and tennis shots and always insist on the **controlled** use of the stick to deaden the ball.

Rapid propulsion of the aerial ball is always useful but essential at penalty strokes, which are covered later, so it is important to practise these skills. Do not underrate the ability of beginners with some ball skill to propel the ball in almost any position. I teach my nine-year-olds, for example, to hit a ball on the half volley reverse stick. I need patience to endure their misses, but it is very rewarding when a player uses the skill to control a bouncing ball from the right at the far goalpost and scores a winner. This is a classic case of what I call 'having expectations' as a coach - the higher your expectations are, the higher the attainment level of your players.

For all aerial shots check that:
• The ball is positioned in front of left foot
• The body is low
• The body weight is transferred from the right to the left
• There is no twist of the foot or body movement.

Passing

Before starting on the major concept of passing, players must be able to push, hit, slap and lift the ball, and control it from left, right and behind. They will have been passing or, better, giving the ball from the first session. The next section is a simple breakdown of basic passing skills which need to be mastered before you can start on coaching the pass.

General principles

Passing is simply the giving of the ball to another team-member or getting it to a place where one of the players in your team will be able to control and take possession of it. It is a way of keeping team possession. It sounds straightforward, but is actually more difficult in hockey than in soccer. The only good pass is a successful one.

The basic qualities of any pass are:
• **Ball speed** which is often undervalued. It is important to stress this first because young players will tend to pass right to left across a defender's open stick and wonder why the ball is consistently given away. Since youngsters do this a lot, the teaching of pace on the ball is useful. A pass is easily intercepted if it is rolled gently about with an opponent near at hand.
• **Direction** is vital as players should be encouraged to pass into a space where another player can intercept it. Remember that left-to-right passes are more difficult to give and much more difficult to receive.

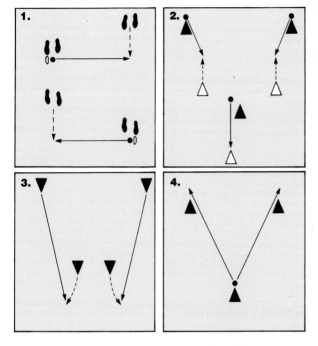

Passes
1. The square pass
2. The back pass or 'drop'
3. Through pass
4. Diagonal passing

• **Timing**, which some say is a natural talent but, if that were true, there would be precious few players. Timing a pass or judging when to give it can and must be taught to players.

The four main types of pass

1. **The square pass** which has been much used, praised and over-stressed in recent times. It is important, however, to insist that the receiver is behind the line of the ball as illustrated above, so as to be able to move onto the ball at pace. Square passes need a fast ball to be effective.

2. **The back pass** which is made immediately behind the player or 45° backwards, and is highly effective but underused. It requires good body movement, and is especially useful to change the direction of attack or maintain possession in defence. This pass is often termed the drop.

3. **The through pass** needs good timing and pace and is generally, though not always, played into space. It is not always directly parallel to the side line but is in an arc of, say, 20° from directly ahead.

4. **The diagonal pass** is a much-maligned pass. It is dangerous, but can be effective if done properly. This pass, left to right, has to be accurate, is often played just behind a defender, and is sometimes lifted. The pass from right to left is fraught with peril and to be successful needs; pace, to beat the interception; lift for the same reason; and disguise to throw the defender off the scent - it is an easy scent to pick up. Do emphasize that this particular pass is often like a cross or centre given to the back foot of the receiver to make a tackle difficult for a defender.

Passing practices

To help you, here are a series of progressive practices from a much wider range of possible practices, to give to your players. Organize them in pairs and interchange their roles.

• **Simple passing**, left to right and right to left. Players should collect the ball on the open side. Stress the need for body movement when passing left to right.

Further practices include passing diagonally, left to right and right to left, and passing square left to right and right to left.

• **Passing through the whole arc**. This can be done with cones or better, players, depending on the space available. Automatically the passer will have to think about body and foot position. Discourage sloppy passing and vary the distance.

• **Basic passing but incorporating the use of a cone** (defender) which has to be avoided.

• **Basic passing behind or in front of an active defender**. This will almost certainly cause problems. Stop the practice if necessary and explain the need to draw or move a defender out of the space needed for the pass. Use a grid ten by ten metres and practise:

- the square pass to left
- the square pass to right (reverse and open side)

More advanced sequence work using an area 30 by 15 metres or, better, 40 by 20 metres create a sequence. Cones or defenders should be some ten metres apart.

Passing practices
1. Square through sequence - players running without the ball.
2. Square through dribble sequence
A always passes square and dribbles
B always passes through and receives.

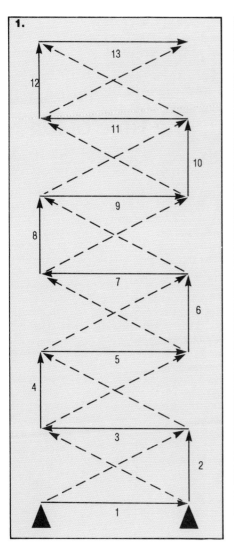

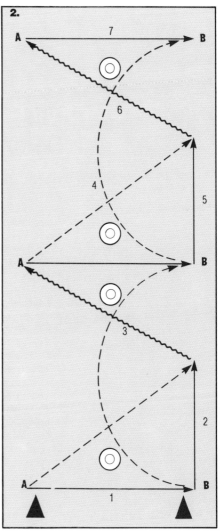

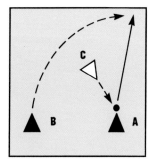

B's running enables A to beat C with through ball.

Sequences include: Square, square, square
Square, through, square
Square, through, dribble.

With these three practices note that you can practise receiving skills as well as a host of others. Get the players to tell you how many skills are included.

Passing: The Role of the Defender

You will need to put over to your players the notion that two players can work in harmony, moving with the ball before passing to draw out a defender, and then passing.

Introduce the concept of the dropped ball, when playing two players versus one. It is possible for the player to drop the ball behind him off either shoulder on command, with the receiver positioned to pick it up with the reverse stick off the right shoulder, or the open side off the left. This practice is good fun but requires a lot of work and good timing.

When using an active defender in practices, coach the thought processes, preferably by question and answer. Get two demonstrators (pick the best players) to help, and ask the group how the passers and defenders can improve a simple two-versus-one situation. For example:

Question: How can the passer make life easier for receiver and vice versa?

Answer: In the form of a demonstration to show how running 'off the ball' (that is, without the ball) can help the man 'on the ball'.

Question: How can the passer throw the defender the wrong way by disguise?

Answer: In the form of a demonstration to show the under-the-arm pass.

Special Types of Pass

Below: Options open to right-winger who has reached base-line.
Bottom: Right-wing attack using active attackers and defenders.

All set-pieces are a sort of pass. The penalty stroke, bully, corner and hit-in are more difficult set-pieces as the passer has to be stationary. The corner and hit-in are covered in more detail in later chapters. How often do we see wingers get to the goal-line and blast the ball into the crowd? It's bad enough in soccer but in a crowded defensive area in hockey and the aerial shot into the 'D' illegal, the centre, or cross, has to be good. The receiver, usually under pressure, needs a sympathetic pass. Wingers or those in that position must look up, pick a man or space, and then give the ball.

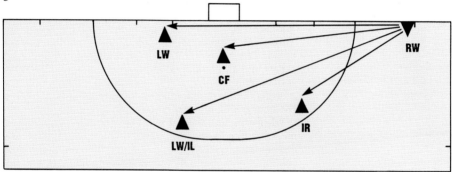

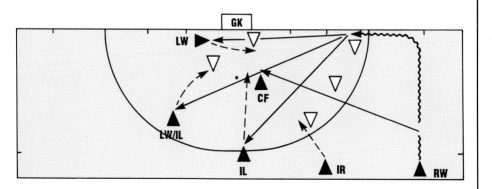

Practices for the cross

• Passing early from the right wing
• Passing late from the right wing, when the winger has reached the base-line
• Passing early from the left wing after pulling the ball back
• Passing late from the left wing, from the base-line and hard on to the open side of the attackers' sticks.

A simple practice routine which offers limitless variations.

Since the left winger has a particularly difficult job, coaches should not be afraid to teach reverse-stick hitting (see Chapter 8). On artificial surfaces particularly this is much quicker than a pull back and hit, and gives defenders, who find it easy on the right, anyway, no time to make the tackle. The Germans teach it young and so can we. I've seen several reverse-stick crosses (and goals!) from ten-year-olds.

You might like to start with wingers in position with a dead ball, then get them, to move from say the 25-yard line using cones as channels to hit down. Then you can fill the circle, to your taste, with defenders and attackers. A good practice is to simulate basketball by allowing attackers only a set time in the circle before they must leave it. In this way you introduce the concept of not standing still, of filling up the space they want empty, and not allowing themselves to be easily marked.

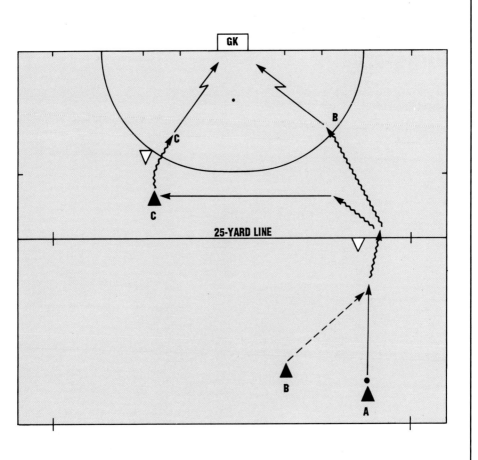

GK

B

C

25-YARD LINE

C

B

A

53

Summary

You can now put together any permutation of the skills. Some examples might be:
• Square pass, control, shot
• Through pass, control by running towards pass. Dummy defender and then shot or another pass
• Beating a player, giving a lifted pass, receiving the return, beating another player, attacking the goal line and centring the ball for another shot
• Aerial ball, control, shot
• Reverse-stick pass, receive the return, reverse-stick centre, or shot at goal.

ELEMENTARY GOALKEEPING

Elementary Goalkeeping

Choosing a Goalkeeper

Find the **gymnast**! That's the best advice I can give to the perplexed coach looking for a player to train as a goalkeeper. Do **not** put your most weighty player in goal - or anyone whose eyes don't immediately light up when you ask the group for a volunteer. You'll probably get several hopefuls, but choose the one with agility. As well as **agility,** the goalkeeper should have **speed, strength,** powers of **concentration** and sublime **confidence,** bordering on arrogance. So sort out your programme to produce this most important player - after all, if he does not make a mistake your team won't lose.

You need to strike a balance in your keeper between natural ability and technique. (Often a second-string soccer keeper will have the necessary qualities.) As far as technique is concerned, you must beware of a youngster becoming a coaching-manual 'model' - doing all the stylish actions but missing the ball. Basically, when goalkeeping, the body weight should never be moving backwards in any position. If it is the next move can't be made quickly and therewill be a loss of balance when making the second, or third save, and so on.

The good goalkeeper should always be in the alert position with the head forward and knees slightly bent, ready for instant movement in any direction. From this alert position, the ball is saved and then cleared by using the foot, preferably, or the stick as a second choice. Either way the ball is cleared quickly and as wide as possible.

The saves that are made high to the left involve hand-use followed by use of the foot or stick to clear. Saves low to the left should be made with the foot, though in the far corner a dive left to save with the glove is desirable - and spectacular. Saves made high to the right still involve the left hand coming over the body as the body arches and then the clearance. Saves made low to the right should be made with the foot, with the head kept over the ball, or, if dealing with a corner, a dive and a stick save - again very spectacular!

The use of the stick above the shoulders in a high save to the right is now permitted.

Right: Clearing to the right
Far right: Clearing with the stick to the left
Bottom: A high save made with a dive to the right.

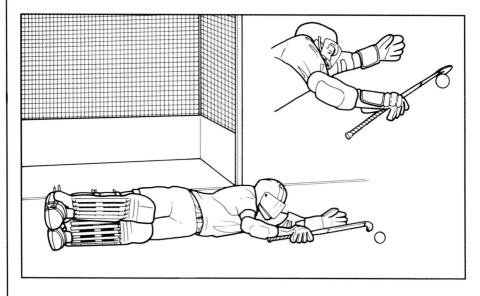

A shot can be blocked by the keeper lying full length across the goal mouth using his stick - in this illustration, on the reverse side as he is reaching to the left.

There is also the save-clear technique where both actions are fused into one, a method largely developed and perfected by Ian Taylor, the Olympic Gold Medallist. The goalkeeper propels the ball away with either foot, kicking with the inside of the kicker or pad through the line of the ball away from the danger zone, with balance all the time and the head positioned as far as possible over the ball. This is an excellent technique but is heavy on the knees and very young players find it difficult. They will also tend to kick with the instep as in soccer, and they must be cautioned about giving away penalty (short) corners by dangerous lifting of the ball, since the rule for keepers is as for players, though you wouldn't believe it sometimes.

The difference in conventional and save-clear techniques is often related to kit. Continental keepers tend to use so-called absorbent kit which means that they have to be able to clear after a save with foot and stick. The rebound quality of modern kit makes this style less necessary, but coaches are advised not to skimp on technique because this kit, particularly the kickers, will not always do the work for them! Goalkeepers have to be able tackle with either foot or the stick, especially in one-to-one situations.

There are occasions when the goalkeeper has to spread to block the shot and cover as much of the goal as possible. This requires good timing, agility and a fearlessness (some say mild insanity is useful and total madness even better!). Make sure the keeper is fully equipped for all these skills to give him maximum protection (and security) from the beginning.

Note
Goalkeeping kit is covered in detail in Chapter 6.

Practices for Goalkeepers

Goalkeeping training is specialized and involves agility exercises, which resemble warm-up stretches except that a good keeper will spend a long time on them. Daily stretching is highly desirable.

The 'sideways shuffle' movement which the goalkeeper uses to manoeuvre around the goal-mouth can be practised in the same way that players practise dribbling moving through a 'slalom'. This practice will increase the keeper's ability to move quickly sideways, which is just as important as forward movement. Goalkeepers must also expect to change position quickly and sort out the angle of shot. A useful quick rule of thumb is to use an imaginary line between ball and the centre of the goal. The keeper stands on it!

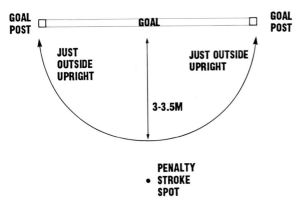

Goalkeeper's movement ellipse

Goalkeeper mobility practice

Right wing and Left wing inject balls, and goalkeeper has to move rapidly to 1, 2 and 3, then on to 4 and 5.

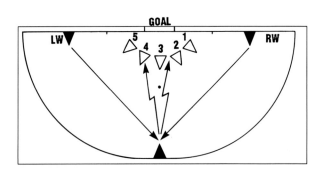

To practise this you will need to simulate the extreme example: a centre from the baseline to the top of the circle. Look at the illustration on page 59. The ellipse that a keeper uses to cover the angles as the ball moves across the circle is shown. Note also that the near post is covered by the nearest leg so a keeper need not lean on the post!

Another useful practice shown to me by John Hurst of England involves a 'points-of-the- compass' practice illustrated opposite. This also improves general movement but is especially useful to replicate short corner work. The keeper should remember to keep the back towards the centre, that is, run backwards after reaching the outer point.

Goalkeepers need to keep fit and should be prepared to do some stamina work such as weekly running routines, but the essential requisite of a top class goalie is leg-power. Weight training is the obvious answer but not always available, so a goalkeeper can be doing some work while others practice, such as step-ups and sit-ups, both before and after 'kitting-up'. (This is a good way to 'soften up' new kit.)

In the real practices you need (i) a sympathetic feeder who need not be a hockey player - an enthusiastic parent perhaps, and (ii) a supply of tennis/hockey balls, at least half-a-dozen but preferably a bucketful.

• Feed balls to each leg by throwing, first at knee height both for save and clear, and then simpler save techniques deliberately practising each foot. Vary the 'width' of the ball. Then increase the power and speed by hitting balls with a stick at fairly close-range. Of course the same 'feed' practices can be used to practice stick saves and glove saves on both sides. It is best to get accurate feed so a fault can be remedied. Do not use feeders who want to blast a ball past the keeper - it is the keeper that is practising, not the attacker.

• Move on to 'rebound' practices which can utilize one, two or three balls and any number of players. Here are just a couple of examples:

1. To coach the keeper in a one-to-one situation, simulating an attacker who has made his way into the circle past a passive defender, position him in the goal mouth, sitting down to start if

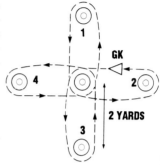

2 YARDS

Points-of-the-compass shuttle run
The goalkeeper runs around the points of the compass, north, south, east and west, but always keeping his back to the centre post.
Rebound practices
Top left: Rapid-fire pressure practice
B or C strikes the ball as soon as goalkeeper has saved shot from A.
Bottom left: A shoots and B, C and D try to score from the rebound.

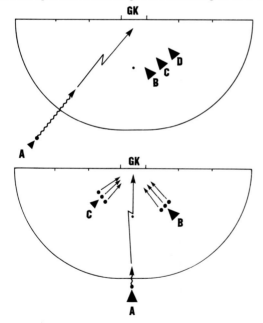

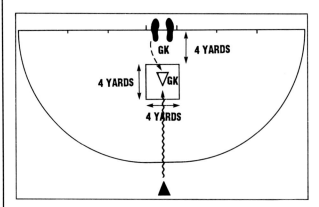

'Sweat box' - an advanced goalkeeper-tackling practice
The goalkeeper sits in his goal with his back to the attacker. The attacker starts on the 25-yard line and when he begins his attack, the goalkeeper gets up, turns and runs into the grid. The attacker tries to beat the goalkeeper in the box. The goalkeeper returns to his line after every attack.

Goalkeeper tackling practice
The attacker tries to beat the goalkeeper without leaving the box.

you want to increase the pressure, when the attacker starts his run. Coaches must supervise these practices to avoid overtaxing the keeper, and make the attacker start his run at various distances outside the circle.

Since June 1989, the practice of lying down to await the first shot is penalized by a penalty stroke. However, provided the keeper is not actually prone at the moment of the shot, he can 'go down' after the strike. Umpires have difficulty with this, but young keepers need not be encumbered by these technicalities.

Lastly, insist at **all times** that the goalkeeper wears his **helmet**.

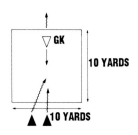

GROUP COACHING AND TEAM SKILLS

Group Coaching and Team Skills

At the outset you ought to realize that this work can do no more than underline the fundamentals. If you want a more in-depth discussion you should consult more advanced manuals (see book list at the back of this book).

General coaching hints when setting up group work include:

• Young beginners like to work hard for short periods
• They like to change 'ideas' frequently
• They need constant encouragement
• Older beginners like to compete and concentrate
• They like to get involved in games quickly which is often why they are less accomplished
• They are less likely to take on a radical or new viewpoint.

So plan your coaching so that everyone gets involved. The reason why small-team games are valuable is because everybody does!

You must decide **why** you are playing a particular game. Either for four-a-side, for example, or for a conditioned game there has to be an **end product**. Let's start by separating conditioned games and small-team practices.

The former are to aid a technique such as passing, whereas the latter are part of a progressive structure which includes two-versus-one play, four-versus-two and so on. The most important concepts of covering, marking and channelling are also covered, taking in both defensive and attacking play.

1. Conditioned Games

There are many of these but here is an example involving three limits on the 'no tackling, no dribbling'game which are the most valuable for demonstrating the basics of covering, passing and other skills described in Chapter 3.

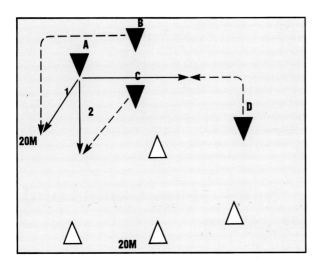

A four-versus-four practice in which three passes are created by the running of B, C and D.

No tackling, no dribbling

Play this in a limited area, say four-a-side, in a twenty-metre square, to develop passing skills. Use the base-line as a goal which is scored by putting the ball on the line under control. Players are not allowed to run with the ball or tackle, but can intercept and run off the ball. This encourages players to run into position for a pass since that's the only way to score! This practice is also useful for teaching covering in defence as shown in the pattern.

Allow a metre or so for control and don't worry too much about the standard rules except obstruction and stick interference.

• Simply use the no-tackling condition as in the practice above, as this increases the passing speed and ensures that the players look before passing.

• Allow dribbling but no tackling, but only permit a dribble for, say, ten metres. This will force players to practise closing-down rather than tackling. This is a valuable constraint as it improves the vision and footwork of defenders, as well as giving attackers an ego-trip!

• Every two passes forward should be followed by one behind, square. Neither tackling nor dribbling are allowed, but interception is encouraged. This is excellent practice for build-up play as well as for defensive techniques such as dealing with the question of how a player reacts when the opposition passes the ball away from him.

You can of course develop these to your own taste and target so that they are not only for fun. You can vary the conditions, the 'absolute' nature (for example by allowing a five-metre dribble), or the number of players, which need not necessarily be the same on each side, to encourage a particular skill. This neatly brings us on to area-practices leading to small-team games.

2. Small Team Games and Practices

In this you can develop the concept of **two players versus one**, fundamental to modern hockey. Four-versus-two and six-versus-four are simply multiples of two-versus-one, at this basic level anyway! Once the two- versus-one idea is established, the small team game improves dramatically, though I would play a three-versus-three or four-versus-four game in my very first practice with beginners at the end of the session.

At an early stage put the whole two-versus-one concept into a game concept by asking players to imagine, for example, that two players are the Inside Right and Right Wing, playing against a Left Half.

In the diagram above, and in practice, a ten-metre square is about right, with the easy option to extend to 20 metres by ten. Using this area, the two players simulating Inside Right and Right Wing try to pass a Left Half, which in theory they should always manage. You can imitate this by setting up sidelines and examples such as Left Half and Centre Half against an attacking Inside Right, a common game situation where a left-side defence is trying to move the ball to the right.

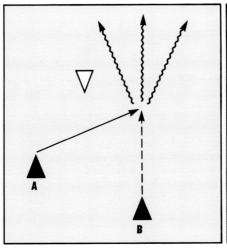 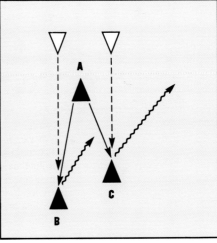

The basic principles of small team practices are that:
• Players in possession should be able to draw the defenders by means of a dummy or a change in the angle of running, to create a space for the pass.
• The second attacker must help support the player on the ball, otherwise the practice will degenerate into a one-to-one situation.
• Players try to pass left to right. It is easier for the receiver on the open side and the ball moves across the reverse of the difficult side of the defender. The receiver is also in a strong position to execute his next move.
• An early pass draws a defender and gives the return pass opportunity, known to all as the 'old one-two'.

It is important to observe here that playing the ball forward or square is not always desirable, particularly if the support runner is not using his wits. Very often attack in the line-astern formation has great advantages, and the ball played backwards off either shoulder pulls the defender into an impossible position. Remember **the most dangerous man on the pitch is the man who has just passed the ball.** The defender will follow the ball, and intelligent running by the player who has just passed will cause great problems.

Above left: A two-versus-one practice in which player B has many options.
Above right A three-versus-two practice in which the ball is played backwards to B or C with subsequent possible moves.

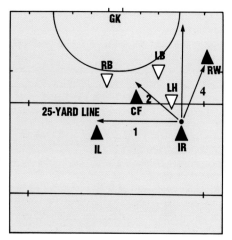

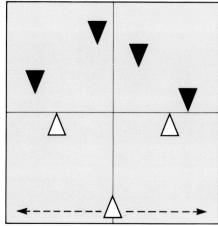

Top left: Four-versus-three practice
The Inside-right with the ball has three options.
Top right: Three-versus-four practice illustrating that the pattern players adopt gives efficient cover

You can probably now see how you can employ these basic concepts in enlarging your practices into four-versus-two, five-versus-three, six-versus-four, six-versus-five and then into six-versus-six or six-a side play.

The basic idea is to create two-versus-one in a particular area (or failing that, one-versus-one) but not one-versus-two, or two-versus-three where the opposition now have more men!

If you are coaching attack, use five-versus-four, four-versus-three or three-versus-two situations to set up a bank of two-versus-one situations and you now have a conditioned game.

If you are dealing with defence, load the dice the other way, with one-versus-two, two-versus-three, three-versus-four then four-versus-four and six-versus-six. At this point the concepts of covering and marking are introduced. We can illustrate these concepts by using a series of progressive practices, remembering to expand the pitch size as six-versus-six situations draw nearer.

• **One-versus-one**: Start with an area of 20 metres (or 15) by ten. The first practice is to establish the recovery angle.

• **One-versus-two**: Use the same size area but the defender should slow up the attackers by keeping on the line of the ball and middle of the goal, using the closing down skills already described.

• **Two-versus-three**: Introduce marking with cover, asking the players to think the problem through. Active learning methods will

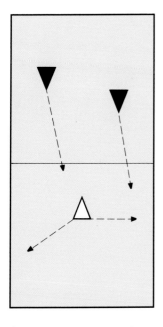

One versus two practice
Two players are delayed by
covering the line of the ball

ingrain the truth! Get them to criticize when relevant. Use the 20 metres by ten format.

• **Three-versus-four**: Use an area 20 metres by 20, or a much wider pitch than previously. The idea here is to have the three operate as a unit, both covering and marking.

• **Four-versus-four**: Use an area 20 metres by 20 again. Here the four defenders provide cover, usually in a sort of diamond shape, and when they get possession, the other four become defenders and you have a four-versus-four game.

• **Six-versus-six**: Use a bigger pitch, say 50 metres by 50, or 40 metres by 40, otherwise congestion starts.

Stress that once the opposition have the ball, all players should defend, and then you can sort out any problem with marking, covering and defending by zone. This is easier applied than the man to man marking much commended by Horst Wein (Chapter 10), but the aim here is to teach covering which is really a sort of zone defence. If you have basketball players use one of them to help you explain!

Summary

The aims and objectives in these progressive practices include:
• Improving the reaction of players to losing the ball so they attack the defence
• Getting players in possession of the ball to gain ground quickly
• Getting players into position to receive a pass
• Encouraging players to understand the importance of their role when not in possession.
• Getting players to support the man with the ball!
• Developing the idea of a player being part of a triangle.

Commend the idea of playing six-a-side or perhaps eight-a-side up to Under-12 level. The players touch a ball more often and one can dispense with off-side and other concepts which are better picked up later and are quite irrelevant to the development of the player.

Indeed on the Continent, particularly in Holland, at Under-10 level six-a-side is normally played and eight-a-side for the ten-to twelve-year-old age group. The growing success of the mini-hockey competition in this country amply repays faith in small-team games. I do almost all my coaching in a Sports Hall 34 metres by 17 and it's quite a surprise to see how quickly the five-a-side skills translate into the eleven-a-side game.

Tips for Coaching in the Game Situation

• Aim to create a unit or team
• Analyze and correct tactical faults
• Put two-versus-one etc into a game context
• Try to avoid confusion in the game by not stopping the game too often
• Adopt the right place to stand on the pitch where you can be heard
• You can 'freeze' the game on command or have frequent two-minute pauses for discussion. If you're lucky, use both a coach on the edge of a pitch and one in a given area.
• Try to work in **ten to twenty-minute periods** with a set aim. One of these could be to test reaction to lost possession. You can do this by playing five-versus-five with forwards defending, or with five who always play in the defence in possession. By getting the forwards to play in the other direction when possession is lost, a ten-versus-five situation is created. It is chaotic to start with but do persevere!

Another good way of testing reaction is to play in limited space, five versus five with two balls. Players have often to pass in attack and watch out for the other ball as well. This practice is very popular with young children and very, very useful. Again give it a few minutes to settle down.

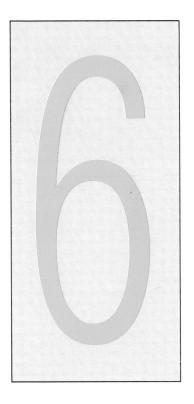

EQUIPMENT

Equipment

It is essential to demand, at the outset, that each player has proper equipment. Sticks should be an appropriate weight for the player, have a thin handle, preferably be two inches wide on the control area, particularly those for the younger player. It is possible to buy a bundle of sticks at a sports shop on a sale-or-return basis or at 'sales'. You can get then sell them to players or ask the club to part-fund them.

Players ought to be made to wear shin-guards, preferably ones which are light but offer ample protection. There are various types available, though generally the more expensive the better the protection.

Clothing must always be suitable for the training session and most youngsters should have waterproofs if training outdoors. Good footwear is vital as smooth soles can be lethal. Sometimes studded footwear is need for heavy or wet grass.

Later in the programme, when fixtures are made, more equipment will be needed. Sometimes you may be able to persuade a local firm to sponsor shirts, for example, but do not forget the guidelines governing the size of a sponsor's name on kit. Shorts of the tennis variety are best and, in fixtures, they should be a uniform colour. Socks again ought to be the same, and plain white is usually safe. Always bear in mind that, good coach that you are, players will drop out and it is unfair to ask for too much expenditure from your pupils.

At some stage it is a good idea to try to get stick-holdalls in the club's colours or have them custom-made, since this helps to create a team atmosphere and sense of belonging, and they keep sticks dry too! While on the subject, advise players to let all kit dry naturally.

Other extras which can be put into a small kit-bag or inside a stick-holdall, include a gum-shield (best made by a dentist), tape for fingers and knuckles and if indoors, stick wear. Some players carry small medi-kits but these are usually international tourists who would also take items like needle and cotton.

I discourage players from wearing gloves except in extremes of temperature, but I always carry some gauze and sandpaper to roughen stick handles as they do get very slippery when it rains.

Goalkeepers' Kit

We have mentioned goalkeepers already but kitting them out is an area where your coaching reputation is at risk. Even my nine-year-old keeper has the very best kit. I know it's expensive but trying to save a few pounds here can be disastrous, in terms of injury and in producing competent keepers. Protect yourself by insisting on the best kit for your goalkeepers and take out an insurance policy.

•**Helmet** (masks are not as good) and a throat protector either attached to the helmet or as a separate item

•**Upper-body protection**: Ice Hockey/American Football shoulder pads and chest protector

•**Abdominal protector** - ensure it is of the best quality

•**Padded shorts** (Ice Hockey), or players' girdle which is difficult to get outside North America but worth the effort. Try phoning stockists of Ice Hockey equipment

•**Elbow pads** to prevent injuries from falls

•**Gauntlets** are much better than padded gloves, and gardening gloves make perfect inners

•**Pads** should be as light as possible, though the lighter they are the more expensive they tend to be. Ensure they are not too small (to avoid thigh injury) or too big (producing immobility)

•**Kickers,** again with total protection and in the lightest possible weight to breed confidence

•**Set of spare straps for pads and kickers**. Beware of Murphy's Law - they are almost bound to break when you are least expecting it

•**Stick**: I recommend an indoor stick since keepers are not going to hit the ball and an indoor stick is light and more easily handled

•**Instructions on care** of all the above and make the keeper look after his kit. Good habits and pride are worth having

•**Spares**: Sometimes keepers like to carry screws and screwdriver with scissors to replace helmet-screws or cut loose thread. Tape is also useful for emergencies and to protect pads and kickers on abrasive surfaces such as shale and sand-fill.

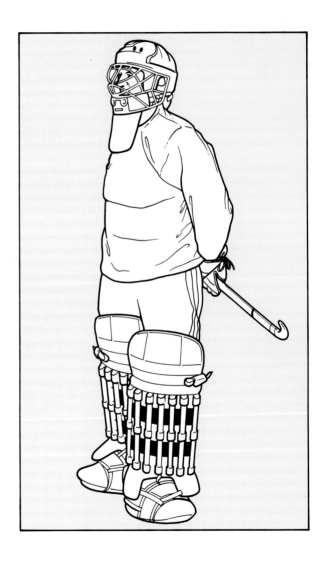

A fully-equipped goalkeeper

Tips
• Make sure the club puts money by for inevitable wear and tear
• Foam (high density) can be obtained from all sorts of shops and easily tailor-made into arm or thigh-protectors with elastic or velcro. Improvisation is practised by all the top keepers simply to prevent injury!

Group Equipment

This was discussed in the formulation of the programme but a detailed list is always of practical use:

•**Cones**: There are two sorts. The older variety, in various sizes as seen by motorway travellers is available from sports equipment suppliers and should not be purloined from the authorities! I prefer the 'mine' variety which are like cones without the centre - that is, with a hole in the centre and about three inches high. They are useful for all sorts of marking and are obviously less bulky. You can carry 50 without any problems, but you will have to buy these as they aren't used on motorways!

•**Bibs**: I'm not a fan of bibs where elastic can stretch and bibs flap about, but they are useful if numbered for selection. A set of shirts plus a mandatory personal white shirt is preferable, in my opinion, and bibs are not inexpensive.

•**First aid kit**: As we said, the club will scratch its collective head but remember that you have a moral (and legal) obligation and good practice demands a kit. The normal Sports Medical Kit will do provided you add ice which is more used than anything else. Reading simple advice from sports physiotherapists is of course a wise move. Don't forget tablets for things like headaches which are more common than injuries. Note a doctor's address and that of the nearest sports physiotherapist for medium and long-term treatment but don't worry about injuries. Keep calm.

•**Balls**: Practice balls, preferably of a distinctive colour, of non-stick, smooth plastic surface are best. Make sure you get more than you need as you'll use them before season's end! I like coaching with mini hockey balls (3 1/2 oz) which are bigger and less likely to cause injury, especially to keepers. They are easier for stick work. Obviously match balls can come from club supplies, and it doesn't matter if they are slightly used. It is always helpful to have a dozen used tennis balls for use in goalkeeper practices.

• **Sundries**: Whistles, are obviously vital and they get lost, so buy three or four at a time. Tape and things like string are useful in case the goal-nets you use are abused or have large holes which can be dangerous. A set of blank postcards is handy to jot down your practice notes in advance!

Also, keep a comprehensive list of players and addresses and telephone numbers you will use frequently. I always carry a Rule Book with me just to check measurements as well as rules.

SET PIECES

Set Pieces

This book can give only a basic introduction so for more advanced techniques refer to the book list in Chapter 10.

Set pieces can be grouped into three categories:

1. Moving a 'dead' ball, in a free hit, a hit-in from side line and a sixteen-yard hit (like goal-kick in soccer)

2. Corners, which have similarities to (1) but involve some special problems

3. Penalty corners, more usually called short corners, which are unique.

1. Moving a Dead Ball

When hitting the 'dead' ball (sometimes called restart) there are certain basic concepts which include:

• Taking the restart quickly, as the sooner the ball is moving the more difficult it is to defend

• Not giving possession away if it is not possible to restart quickly

• Seeking variety. Always have a support player close for a short ball and a 'long' option

• Deciding, early on, whether movement by your support players can create a space

• Seeking disguise and trying not to 'telegraph' intentions.

Now that we have some general points, how does moving a dead ball affect play when the player is in the attacking area, say, near the opponent's circle? You'll know that in hockey and soccer the wastage rate is high! You need to have one or two simple moves rehearsed which take into the account that the area is small and full of players, making it difficult to see the opening. You can use your two-versus-one skills quite effectively, but also get your players to dream up new moves. This is one of the best occasions for active player learning! In my experience players like to think up ideas and try them out, and you test their understanding of the basic principles when discussing them. Who is in charge at the free hit? Who does the thinking? Needless to say your advice on 'passing' skills is essential as it is easier to defend a dead ball. Movement 'off the ball' is crucial and there are many variations.

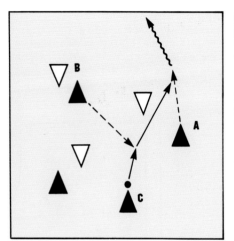

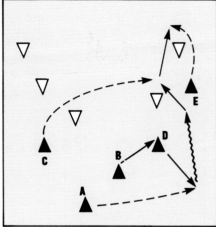

Above left: A two-versus-one practice in which player B has many options.
Above right: A three-versus-two practice in which the ball is played backwards to B or C with subsequent possible moves.

In the defensive area the trick is not to give the ball away. The opponent does not have to travel far to reach a good shooting position. The defence should put themselves under pressure to perform well.

What basic choices does a player have at the 16-yard restart or free hit?

• A short pass to a colleague who then moves forward to get the ball into midfield

• A pass to Right or Left Winger who needs to do a lot of work to evade his marker

• A direct pass to, say, Inside Right or Left - but again they will have to shake off markers

There are of course, many others but a good coach can 'winnow' ideas from the players. Teach them the basic concepts and emphasize that it is a crime to give the ball away!

Sideline hit or push-in
Bottom left: A two-versus-one sideline option
Bottom centre: A and B create a two-versus-one situation
Bottom right: Left wing running into space

Sideline hit or push-in

The same principles should be followed as before but you have only a 180° arc so players should:

• Take no silly risks especially near their own goal
• Support the injection of the ball with players to keep possession, remembering that the 'hit-in' can be taken like a free hit since the opposition have only to be five yards away
• Use the two versus one concept.

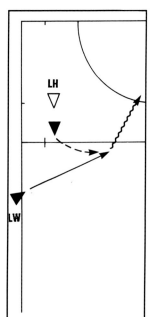

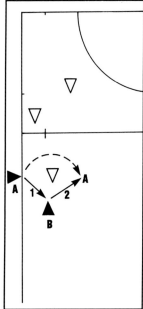

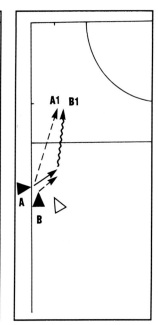

2. Corners

Corners
Five possibilites

Corners are simply a variety of hit like the hit-in or side-line ball. This is because the basic rules for free-hits apply, for example, with opponents only five yards from the hit. However, corners have the special constraints of being taken in confined space, and the ball must be played on the ground since a ball cannot be lifted into the circle. Add to that the number of players in the shooting area, often numbering seventeen or eighteen, and it becomes a dead-ball 'blast' into the mass of players. In addition as there's only 90° of angle it can lose its potency if it isn't planned.

You still keep the option of a man close, and try to position players (who, of course, will try to lose their markers) to utilize the various angles. The diagrams show the situations well, particularly the need for intelligent running off-the-ball.

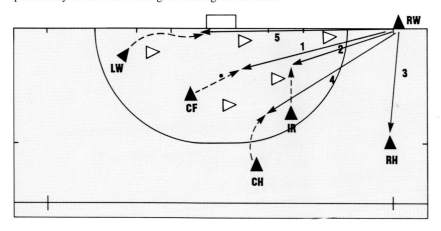

Corners
Right: The Centre-Half and Inside-Left create a pass by movement.
Bottom right: The Left-Half has options if the Inside-Left draws the defence by running.

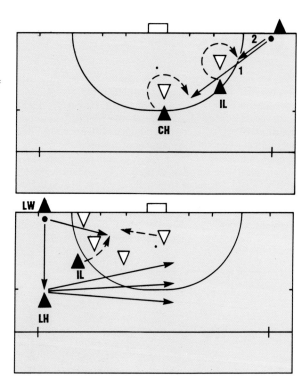

3. Penalty (or short) Corners

Penalty (or short) corners are a means of winning the game, and bad defensive work at them is a quick way of losing one! The idea is a half-penalty so the dice are supposed to be loaded in favour of the attack!

In this set-piece you should look for your players with what are called secondary skills - that is, choose the cricketer with the best stick-stop to stand ready at the top of the circle and involve your

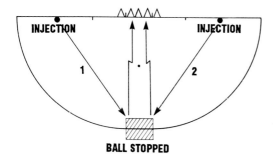

Penalty (or short) corners
A simple outline

best striker for the shot, even if he is the sweeper. The Centre Forward may well be the fastest man in your side, so use him to be the initial runner out to the top of the circle. Be radical, with no pre-conceived ideas about players.

The simple mechanics of the short corner are illustrated above. The ball has to be played at least ten yards from either upright and then stopped, for a shot at goal. The defenders must preferably stop a shot being made and clear the ball out of the circle or, at least, then prevent a goal if a shot is made.

The major defensive 'problem' areas are illustrated but there are various ways to minimize the danger by using the essential defence team of goalkeeper and four defenders. The standard routine is to employ a first man out, who runs out when the ball is played and tries to gain possession or interfere at the top of the circle. A second runner comes out either right or left to cover the slip or the ball played sideways from the top of the circle. One or both of the remaining players become 'post' men standing about two metres out, balanced in line to save balls wide of the goalkeeper. The goalkeeper may well have come three or five metres off the goal-line, but at time of shot must be balanced and not 'on the move'. Goalkeepers are often better on their left side, since the right foot which 'pushes' them to the left is usually stronger. Some goalkeepers, therefore, opt for only one man on the right post, and send the third man out to 'clear up' rebounds, the ball slipped back to the short-corner taker (who is often called 'injector').

Penalty (or short) corners

Variations in short corners from the defensive point of view (1) and (2), and from the attacking point of view (3).

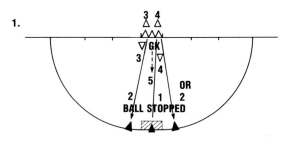

1.

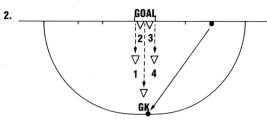

2.

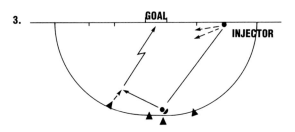

3.

There are other ploys. Goalkeeper and post men stand only a few metres out and the two other 'runners' allow the shot, but are better placed to clear the rebound (assuming of course,that the ball has not gone in the goal!), and it's very common for a goal to come from the second or third shots.

We have already spoken about the practice of goalkeepers lying down, being struck by the ball and defenders clearing. This is not advisable for schoolboy or club goalkeepers other than at the highest level.

How do you set up practices? The answer is to **build them up** piece by piece. Practice defence first. To save time don't 'inject' the ball from the baseline but bring it on the field, from the mark at the top of circle, for a seven-metre push. This limits error, and you can also practise attacking penalty corners, particularly the stick-stop and hit-share between two players, and you will have created more opportunities to deploy your players.

Coaching Set Pieces in Defence

When coaching set pieces in defence:
• Cover the percentages, the dangerous areas of the circle
• Calculate where you prefer the shot to come from, so as to deploy your defenders, probably to the left
• Runners must not block the view of the keeper or run so fast they can only stop at the 25-yard line! They won't be able to help much from there!
• The more moves the attack makes, the longer and the less effective it will be, provided your unit defence reacts as you have practised
• Deploy your best players for the job, and pay individual attention to the job. It is always tempting to look at the keeper, but do look at one or two specific roles per practices
• Try to get everyone involved, with two or three groups practising simultaneously.

Coaching Set Pieces in Attack

In attack, the coach must again practise the moves but be insistent upon certain basics which help improvisation - for example, if the shot is spoiled an attacker must try to keep a stick on the ball. This is especially important on artificial grass as it is very difficult to dispossess a player and the attacker may yet be able to shoot.
• A shot from the top of circle is the best angle but attracts more defenders
• Shots from wide are sometimes easier to make but more difficult to score from
• Simple, well-executed moves are still lethal
• Inventive peculiar ploys may well work once, but not too often
• The more complex the routine, the more likely something will go wrong
• Remember the rules. The ball must be stopped.

Practising penalty corners stretches a coach and there are many pitfalls. Beware of having too many players inactive or practising too many skills simultaneously, and make sure you have separate practices for the defending and attacking of short corners.

Build up your routines stage by stage. For example, the breakdown of practices for the attacking corner are:
1. Practise injection and stick-stop without a final shot
2. Practise the above with the shot but without defenders and goalkeeper
3. Practise the above with the other attackers but still no defence
4. Practise the above but add the goalkeeper
5. Practise the above but add 'post men'
6. Practise the above with the complete defence but passive reaction
7. Practise the above but get the attack to compete with defence (you can have a little competition, but not too many shots).

You can create a similar list for practising defensive corners, using 'dummy' shots to position your players so that they can practise their roles in the various attacking moves.

IMPROVING THE INDIVIDUAL

Improving the Individual

This chapter sets out to describe briefly some of the finer points of the skills already described. David Whitaker in his excellent book *Coaching Hockey* describes it as 'grooving' the skill. This chapter takes the form of a checklist of the hockey skills which the coach should try to groove into his players. The latter part gives the coach some simple ideas on working on fitness for hockey.

Passing Communication Skills

Passing is not just a mechanical process of moving a ball. Good passing involves good communication, that is the players think, talk and look. Eye contact between players is the most desirable since it tells the opposition little, whereas a call can be heard easily. Players must be encouraged to signal intentions by eye contact and by pointing the stick to where they want the ball so making the passer's job easier.

Calling is important and must be demanded early but do put a stop to bad calling or too much of it. There is some dreadful calling in other sports with so many players demanding the ball that the unfortunate passer is totally confused. An early call goes with the concept of looking **before** control (Chapter 3) and the next pass will be quicker because the ball will be on the end of the stick for a fraction of a second only.

Stress also that while running with the ball, the body should be as upright as is possible, with the eyes looking for the pass. Practise this particularly with the contact dribble. This is especially relevant on artificial surfaces.

The basic position of the reverse-stick hit.

The Grip

The player will by now have realized that there is more than one grip! Jab tackling, already discussed, requires a different grip to say, hitting or the Indian dribble, but this progression from the first lesson has never bothered players. Once the left wrist is used to hold the stick in one hand it is a good idea to teach the Jab Dribble. This is a one-handed skill, basically jabbing the ball forward on a line running outside the left foot. This skill, another one handed one, is especially valuable on synthetic surfaces since the ball can be lifted over the flat stick. The ball can then be brought back on to the strong side, again with one-hand. This is a fairly advanced skill but it seems to me that since nine-year-old German players do it as a matter of course, we must treat it almost as a basic skill. It is difficult and a slalom practice is particularly appropriate.

Reverse-stick hit and push-slap

Propelling the ball from left to right using the reverse stick is now a basic skill, particularly on artificial surfaces where it is easier to manipulate the ball or when the general level of tackling skills is such that it is best to hold on to the ball for as long as possible using the reverse-stick stroke to quickly re-position the ball and pass it on.

Accurate hitting from the left, particularly for left-wing centring, is a marvellous asset since it makes a right-side defender's job very difficult.

The ball is opposite the left foot and shoulder as if for the open-side hit. To slap or push a ball, the same applies but with hands apart, though the ball speed will generally, though not always, be lower.

If the player wishes to lift the ball, the coach can allow him to hit opposite the right foot. This can be effective in a shooting context if it is otherwise impossible to get the ball 'strong' in time.

Hitting and Pushing off the Right Foot

Players will not always get the time to line the ball up for a hit off the front or left foot. As Sean Kerly (probably the best Centre-Forward in the world) says, surprise snap-shooting is the key and he can hit the ball with great power with his weight on the rear or right foot. Frankly, this is not an advanced skill: it is just a little more difficult. You can easily assimilate it into a practice - for example, when coaching shooting why not ask players to hit the ball with their weight on the rear foot? It's best to start with a static practice. Watch individual players for head position which still requires to be over the ball if possible, and there should be arching of the back, as well as great use of the wrist.

Coach the use of the bottom (right) hand to propel the stick head through the ball, so limiting the backswing. The basics are as for the standard hit or push but watch for:-
• Weight
• Head position
• Wrist movement.

Use the skill then in a moving practice, reminding players to overtake the ball if it is in front of them. Follow this up by practising the skill, snap-shooting from crosses coming at 90° to the line of shot at goal, for example.

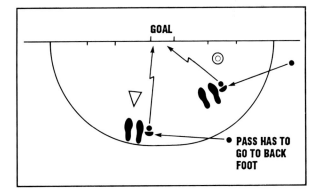

Shooting off the wrong foot using defender or cone

These skills are often called 'wrong foot' skills, since normally a player propels the ball with weight on the front or left foot. In reality, in modern hockey, there is no such thing as a wrong foot. Early propelling of the ball is essential, and since the ball travels faster and further on synthetic pitches, the 'power' of the standard hit is often not required. These are important concepts: as is the need for ball speed.

Channelling

This is an important part of unit defence and is a kind of 'group closing down'. It essentially consists of a defender forcing an attacker into a channel so that a second defender has an easy tackle. It may, of course, take two or three channels to deprive the attacker of the ball, and, thereby, eliminate the danger. The idea is to force an attacker on to the 'open' tackling side. I use the word 'ambush' which seems to be immediately understood by youngsters and describes very accurately what channelling is.

Practices are best done in an area 20 metres by ten metres. Simply play three players versus three, with the task of the defenders being to force the player with the ball as far left as possible.

Remember that channelling is a group skill, while shadowing is where one player manoeuvres another into a weak position and is part of the skill of closing down, already discussed.

Secondary Skills

If you are going to be a winning coach these are vital. So many games are lost because of poor work at penalty corners, and in penalty stroke 'shoot-outs'! I know that I've lost at least six tournament gold medals because of failure at penalty strokes so I write with feeling!

We have already examined penalty corners so we can confine this section to the strokes. The secrets to good strokes are:
• Power
• Placing
• Disguise
• Pressure - how to withstand it.

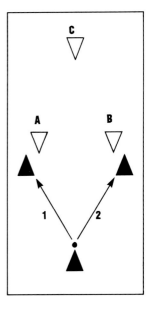

Channelling
A and B channel attacker onto face of player C. A and B promote pass 1 to left wing or pass 2 to the right.

Penalty stroke
In the penalty stroke, both shoulders are open and the body should be kept low throughout.

○

When attacking it is crucial that the player learns to keep his shoulders open from the beginning. If the left shoulder or the feet are not pointing towards the right-hand post, it's going to be very difficult to put the ball to the keeper's left, your right, and this gives him hope. You can always play the ball to the left hand side 'under the arm' because the weight (power) is still correct.

The player should decide where he is going to put the ball and remember the optimum positions. The eyes and head should be kept over the ball. Remember the rule: you are allowed one step, but 'dragging' the back foot, provided it stays on the ground, is not classified as a 'step'.

The power at the point of the stroke is important. Stress the use of the body and the need to get low. If low you can still keep the ball low but you also have the option to lift it.

Ask the taker to work out the factors affecting his decision. Is the goalkeeper very tall, for example? If he is, then the hard low stroke into the corner can be a 'killer'.

Now test your coaching skill:
• Can you pre-select a good stroke-taker?
• Can you make him 'isolate' himself mentally?

One of my best stroke takers is quite fiery on the pitch but ice-cold when taking strokes. To prepare him, tell him to imagine there is nothing else in the world so not only is he totally relaxed, but also his mind is totally concentrated on the task in hand in a sort of 'anaesthetized limbo'!

Finally, if your player has successfully taken strokes, by all means let him carry on. Remember though that, as a coach, it is your duty to the learner to coach him in the correct technique. If the learner is young, technique will help him overcome weak wrists and little body power. Eccentricities are fine if they occur naturally and work, but do not teach them.

Fitness, Training and Running Skills

It is one of the easiest pitfalls for a coach to demand too much physically of young players, so your first consideration must be to consider the age of your group. Are they before puberty? Are they a varied group?

The National Coaching Foundation have published an excellent set of DO's and DON'T's which apply to hockey and all other sports. It is helpful to list the importance of these before discussing general fitness, specific exercises and the pre-game warm-up.

Points to consider over the whole season:
• Be sensible in your expectations
• Be aware of physical development and types it is not age that always counts. Tall thin players, for example, often tire quickly.
• Emphasize skill. The least mature players will mature will good skills
• Encourage players to recognize their physical limitations as it helps them to come to terms with them.

To generate general fitness in your players, use both aerobic (using oxygen) and anaerobic (working without oxygen) exercises, but take great care when putting youngsters through their paces. There is no real bonus to be gained from demanding long distance running of your very young players, or even twelve to fifteen-year-olds. There may be little point, in fact, in asking them to pursue exercise outside training. You will find that in their busy, active lives they do more than enough exercise anyway.

The problem with hockey is that low-speed, long-distance running is not really applicable to the game and at some stage the anaerobic work which demands sudden bursts of energy has to be practised. Do NOT demand this from youngsters. If you are a good coach they will give you all they've got and will not need to be trained to do so. Older players can build up the muscular strength required by weight training, but only under expert guidance.

Speed is obviously vital but in hockey most running is for bursts of seven to 15 metres, so acceleration or how fast a player

---

During practices

DO
• Develop a good general programme
• Emphasize learning skills
• Start gently and gradually increase effort
• Always warm down
• Keep children WARM in cold weather
• Provide liquids for hot weather
• Encourage good eating and sleeping habits

DON'T
• Do adult training programmes
• High-intensity work
• Organize warm-ups which are themselves tiring
• Use weights work except under expert advice
• Do over-long work or indulge in what I call 'heroics' - seeing how far children will go before they crack. This is little short of criminal coaching.

can 'take-off' is even more essential. A young player will run no more than two or three miles during a match and almost all of it will be between seven and fifteen metres in distance. Personally, in acceleration work, I advise training with stick and ball, since I think that introducing a skill with a training run increases the interest and therefore commitment.

Sprinting should be used sparingly and rarely with the very young, but you can help running skills. Hockey players of all ages rarely have time to get into a long sprinter's stride but they can be shown how short, fast-paced acceleration (as used by a sprinter out of the starting blocks) is useful. Training players of all ages to run smoothly, with little shoulder movement and with the stick held in the right hand at the point of balance is worthwhile. During normal training sessions use running exercises and make a point, after a general introduction, of explaining good running technique. Talk to players individually and quietly, since they are often peculiarly sensitive about it.

Specific Exercises

Shuttle running, and running with stick and ball, are always beneficial in hockey training as is anything to strengthen wrists. Again - one must be careful with very young players.

Shuttle runs can be done with stick and ball and I prefer to use seven, ten and 15-metre distances, sometimes going to 20 metres. Remember to allow a decent rest time between each exercise, varying this according to the physical development of the players rather than age. I sometimes have three groups who do the same shuttles but with differing rest-periods.

In general practice it is easy to encourage what in hockey is deficient generally, that is, change of pace. Exercises like dribble runs, for instance can be used to great effect. Ask the players to do three metres slowly, five metres accelerating in pace, five metres slowing down and three metres with a quick burst of speed to try and encourage this quality. It is not only useful, but crucial in the skill of beating a player in a one-versus-one situation.

Muscles can be strengthened by older players using commercial products in a gymnasium and under expert guidance, or by using a simple home-made, but not too heavy, weight. Attach a weight to a piece of rope about one metre long. Fix the other end to a piece of wood about half a metre long, which can be easily gripped in both hands, one at each end. Move the wood through the hands and 'wind up' the weight, then wind it down. This exercise strengthens wrists and must be done regularly for short periods.

Further general strengthening exercises include press-ups, squat thrusts, trunk curls and squat jumps, but these should only be done after a proper warm-up.

Exercises to improve flexibility and dexterity are given below, but do remember that English hockey needs athletes and far too often the athletic nature of the game is understated. Hockey players need to change pace and direction quickly, so players need to develop a high nimble factor!

Exercises include:
• Running and touching the ground occasionally with the hand without stopping
• Running sideways (very important) and changing the leading shoulder regularly, and running backwards.
• Running with crossover steps, rather like a fast polka! This is particularly hilarious and is used by Mike Hamilton, the England Under-21 Coach, before breakfast.

Finally, it is interesting to note that the involvement of athletics coaches in hockey, not only on the Continent but in Ireland and England, is an important development and you should be aware of at least some basics.

Warm-up as part of pre-match training

We have discussed the role of the warm-up in practice session, but it also has a part to play in general pre-match, fitness preparation.

I divide the warm-up into two parts: first the players spend five to ten minutes on their own doing their own running and prepare themselves mentally, then I take a group warm-up to promote team-togetherness.

Before the match

• Arrive at ground one hour before game
• Changing and checking kit - 15 minutes
• Team talk varying in length between five to 15 minutes, depending on the age of the team

• Individual warm-up with gentle running, personal stretching, and time to mentally prepare for the match - ten minutes
• Group warm-up
  (a) Stretching and running - five minutes
  (b) Ball and stick-skills practice, as well as practising penalty corners etc - 15 to 25 minutes (according to time available).

After the match

Group 'warm-down' to relax muscles after work, including gentle running and sometimes 'chat' from the captain about what went right and wrong. This needs to be done not too late after the game: youngsters forget quickly.

It's handy to use your captain to lead the warm-up and warm-down. It increases his esteem and provides an opportunity for him to show his leadership qualities (and you can find out if you picked the wrong person!). I do not like being involved in this after the first event when I've had to show the players what is required.

One last tip: vary the training and running routines. Essentially training is repetitive and has a built-in boredom factor. It's your job to ring the changes as far as possible and, above all, **make training fun**.

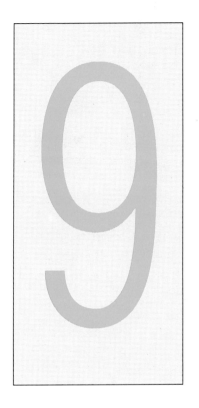

COMPETITION IN HOCKEY

Competition in Hockey

Let us assume you've now got to the position of playing your first match against another club or school. I always recommend you fix an away game at a sufficient distance to make a day out for the players, especially if they are youngsters. This is not so important if players are above, say, fourteen years of age.

Why organize an away match? First it's easier for you: the other club has the venue, teas etc to organize, you just have to deal with transport and kit and hopefully, as it is a day out, you may get help from parents. Try to choose a venue where the players will be welcomed in a spirit of fun for their first game as they are bound to be nervous.

Don't talk about hockey until the one-hour-arrival mentioned in Chapter 8 but then get them to concentrate until after the match when you do something else. When I first assembled an Under-11 team, I decided to go from Wotton-Under-Edge to Havant Hockey Club, for all these reasons. I knew the welcome we'd receive, could introduce them to a Great Britain player (very good psychologically because it does not happen in other sports too often), and Portsmouth Naval Base was nearby for a visit afterwards. The hockey went well, though few players could remember the result by the following week, but above all the day out was **fun**. If you get this **first impression** right, then you'll have created hockey enthusiasts for life and you'll be helped in coaching. So it is worth taking a great deal of care over this first event. If you can't travel, make sure the day is fun, anyway.

I want to note here the great importance of how you prepare your team, whether it be for Mini-hockey, seven-a-side or a full eleven-a-side. You need to prepare them psychologically but don't be frightened, it's not difficult. All you must do is:
• Help establish mutual trust between players
• Choose a captain with leadership qualities who is rated by team
• Build up self-esteem in all your players
• Gain the trust of your players
• Make sure all the players are told, in outline, what they need to remember - and keep it simple.

At half-time do not complicate matters. Boost confidence, analyze general problem, such as, which side of the pitch is being underused, and specific individual ones using a variety of 'tones' to speak to your players. Some will need soothing, some will need a push - your coaching skill is to decide which is required by whom!

After the game, relax the players, and then switch off. Of course, if it's a tournament you need to adjust your methods. If possible I would thoroughly recommend triangular matches (between three teams). There will be plenty of hockey played, especially if you have sixteen in a squad, it is more fun, and gives you future contacts.

Tournaments and Festivals

Suppose you wish to put on your own Mini-hockey or full-team festivals. Here are some guidelines:

Philosophy: Players must enjoy it

Advice: Delegate and involve others in the organization. Keep it within your abilities and ask others who have experience to help you.

Administration: Plan it thoroughly. There is nothing worse than a badly -run day.

Format:
• Full team or not?
• All day or not?
• Number of teams?
• Changing facilities?
• First Aid?
• Catering problems?
• Length of game: pool or round robin?
• Umpires: who and how many?
• Who does what? List people?
• Parking: Catering: Umpire Organizer
• Liaison people: programme and paperwork

• Costings - who pays for what?
• Sponsorship? see Chapter 10
• Check deadlines, don't let them overrun
• Emergency arrangements, for example, in case of bad weather or a team fails to appear
• Tournament referee, or whose decision is final.

Check information to guests:
• Time
• Venue; provide maps
• Colours
• Rules
• Costs
• Age groups
• Cancellation phone number

They need to have this information at least three weeks in advance as they need to circulate the information. It is even better to give a month's notice.

Decide on the nature of the competition. Is it a festival? Do you want a cup? I strongly believe for Under-11's that a festival is preferable. For children under thirteen, don't worry about 'mixed' hockey: boys have not physically advanced on girls so there's no problem.

Check on the day that you have a trouble-shooter. Especially if you are a team manager as it is not fair on your team to get yourself involved in anything else.

Check after the event:
• Letters of thanks are sent
• There is a review and debrief
• Sponsors are kept happy.

Umpiring

In the game and tournament situation the biggest problem is umpiring. First see if you can involve players' parents. Adults are often worried about umpiring and the possible hassle they may get from the players on their decisions. Tell them that you have coached your players never to answer back, and make sure that you do.

You can run a one- or two-evening course to create adequate umpires for very young players. They do it on the Continent and in Holland sixteen- to eighteen-year-old players have to do an umpiring course. It's a way in which players can put back something into a club and it also makes them appreciate the problems of umpires.

Introduce an umpiring element into your programme. Contact the local County umpires organization either through a local telephone directory which should have the County Secretary's name, and details or through the Hockey Association or All-England Womens Hockey Association (see Chapter 10).

Checklist for unqualified umpires

• Use commonsense in 'feet' rule
• Use strict umpiring where safety is involved when, for example,sticks are used dangerously and the ball lifted
• Demand good conduct
• Educate players in the obstruction rule and stick interference.
• Forbid 'wild' play
• Umpire sympathetically: the players are probably struggling with the skills anyway!

Do remember to keep competition within your overall aim of educating players. There are important reasons for not overstressing the element of competition. It is not a personal evaluation of the coach, because a coach with an indifferent pool of talent may work wonders in drawing a game. Another coach who has an impressive pool may well be not doing well even though games are being won.

The question the umpire should always bear in mind is 'What is my aim and am I achieving it?

Safety and injury prevention

I include this here because it's in the game situation, where supervision is only from touch-line, that the risk is highest. Injury-prevention is achieved in two ways: through a proper warm-up, which has already been covered, and play with a high skill level content.

Coaches must be prepared to eradicate the following bad habits:
• Dangerous use of the stick, either high or wide. Encourage the short backlift and locking of the wrist
• The lifted ball - it must be lifted into space

• Control of the lifted ball - it should be allowed to drop
• Umpires need to blow the dangerous aerial early
• Tackling: avoid wild tackling and encourage the keeping of the stick head near to the ground
• Do not allow tackling from behind
• If a youngster's wrists are weak, be careful of one-handed play
• Ensure that players are at least level or their goal-side before tackling.

In Practices
• All ball movement should travel parallel otherwise injury will occur
• Don't allow fiddling with the ball while others are listening to the coach
• Don't allow players to do anything after a whistle is blown, and blow the whistle loudly and briefly. It is amazing how many people don't hear a whistle, especially if the pitch is near a road.
• Insist that everyone always wears the proper equipment in practice - that means shin guards and full goalkeeper's gear. Gum shields are also a good idea
• Insist on instant reaction to your commands
• Don't allow unsupervised mass practice, and remember to have your First Aid Kit handy, together with a phone, so that you can take action at once. But there is no need to be alarmed about this: normal commonsense will guide you through a crisis.

HOW WELL AM I DOING?

How Well Am I Doing?

The best way to analyze your performance is to ask yourself a set of questions. Remember that you start with a lot of plus points - and coaching, whatever your faults whereas others are still simply talking about it.

Ask yourself the following questions:

1. Do I coach to get (a) a high level performance?
   (b) to give fun?
   (c) to help children?
2. Do I put child and athlete above coaching and winning?
3. Children do sport to learn, make friends, have fun, and achieve. Have I helped them do all of these?
4. Do any of the following adjectives apply to my coaching generally, not just in a bad moment: pretentious; negative; unpredictable; chatty; unemotional; over-complicated; blame-obsessed? If you're none of these you're destined for great things!
5. Children like coaches who are: knowledgeable; friendly; authoratitive; interested in the whole person; responsive to good or bad performance; encouraging; decisive; organized; demonstrative and willing to show the player how! Are you all of these? If so ... excellent!
6. Check that you can answer all the following:
   - Do you know why you coach?
   - Are you aware of your influence?
   - What do the youngsters want?
   - Do you teach?
   - Do you provide fun?
   - Are you challenging them?
   - Do you show approval often enough?
   - Do you look at what you did during the last session?
   - Do you ask them what they like?
   - Do you improve your own performance by learning?
   - Do you enjoy coaching? If not, don't!
   - Are you predictable, fair and firm?
   - Are you over-critical?
   - Do you sometimes ignore them?
   - Do you sometimes blind them with science?

• Do you go over the top and lose credibility?
• Above all: are you yourself?

All these questions are a simple way of evaluating performance. I doubt whether you can answer all the above to your satisfaction, and you can console yourself that young people are forgiving and they do like to see human frailty (but not too much) in their coach.

Of all the above, I believe **predictability** is the single most important quality. The chances are that you'll have communication problems with someone, but youngsters will tolerate a lot if they feel secure. This means your behaviour should be predictable. Everyone fears the unknown and the unpredictable is the unknown.

Take heart, however, and don't over-criticize yourself. Your self-esteem is important to your coaching group, even more than it is to you. Good luck and carry on the good work!

Where Do I Go Now?

No-one who is any good at coaching lets time stand still, and these days there are many sources of further assistance in the form of people and organizations and written material.

The game at the junior level is run by two organizations. The Hockey Association with its partner the English Schools Hockey Association (no longer limited to boys at an affiliated school) deals with boys' hockey. For girls, the All-England Womens' Hockey Association through its Director of Coaching, provides similar resources.

These offices provide information about:-
• Coaching and coaching qualifications
• Club coaching
• Videos
• Insurance for coaches: public liability insurance is a must if you are not within the school framework
• Rose Award Skills scheme, a powerful incentive for youngsters

• Umpiring
• Hockey Association and All-England Womens' Hockey Association
• Coaching Associations
• Availability of Senior Staff and Regional Coaches to run sessions for you
• Regional and National Centres of Excellence
• Divisional Chief Coach's register of qualified coaches.

One of the best guides for new coaches is *Helping Hockey* obtainable from the Hockey Association Coaching Office. This includes advice on Mini-hockey and coaching in general, including practical assistance for everyone involved. The *Helping Hockey* booklet also includes 'The Common Approach to the Introduction of Hockey' issued by the Hockey Association and All-England Womens' Hockey Association.

Rule books can be obtained from the offices of the Hockey Association or All-Englands Womens' Hockey Association. Both these bodies are authoritative, andholding lists of affiliated clubs, through counties, divisions and regions. They should be consulted about problems other than coaching; for these the Coaching Offices are more appropriate.

The English Schoolboys Hockey Association is now part of the Hockey Association, and its Secretary provides (as does the HockeyAssociation) information on school and youth organizations, such as Under-13 and Under-11 Mini-hockey.

Addresses

Hockey Association
Coaching Office,
6 St Johns
Worcester
WR2 5AH
0905 426009

Hockey Association
16 Northdown Street
London
N1 9BG
01-837 8878

All-England Womens' Hockey
Association Coaching Office
2nd Floor
10 Parsonage Street
Dursley
Gloucestershire
0453 48096/7

All-Englands Womens'
Hockey Association
Argyle House
29-31 Euston Road
London
NW1 2SD
01-278 6340

Honorary Secretary
Hockey Association Schools
and Youth Committee
16 Clover Drive
Hardwicke
Gloucester
GL2 6TG

National Coaching Foundation
4 College Close
Beckett Park
Leeds
LS6 3QH
0532 744802

Publications

Useful publications for further study are:

Charlesworth and Hatt, *The Young Hockey Player*, Angus and Robertson

Clarke, Trevor, *Hockey Teaching and Playing*, Lepus

Glencross, Denis, *Hockey for Men and Women*, Rigby

Poole, Geoff, *Better Hockey for Boys*, Kaye and Ward

Slocombe and Ward, *Indoor Hockey*, A & C Black

Wein, Horst, *The Advanced Science of Hockey*, Pelham Books

Wein, Horst, *The Science of Hockey*, Pelham Books

Whitaker, D.B., *Helping Hockey*, H A Coaching Office

Whitaker, D.B., *Coaching Hockey*, Crowood Press

There are other books on hockey as a game, not specifically from a coaching angle. These include:

Moore, Chris, *Duel in the Sun*, Garrod

Moore, Chris, *Autumn Gold*, Harrow Press

The National Coaching Foundation produces some excellent books - particularly the Introductory Study Pack, available from

HOW WELL AM I DOING?

the Hockey Association Coaching Office or National Coaching Foundation.

Mini-hockey rule books are obtainable from the Hockey Association Coaching Office.

For umpires there are the following publications:

Selman, Paddy, *The Guide for the Hockey Umpire*

Lilburne, M. T., *Indoor Hockey - A Guide for Umpires*

Magazines are of excellent quality but few in number:

Hockey Digest, Unit 6, Aladdin Workspace, 426 Long Drive, Greenford, Middlesex UB6 8UH

Hockey Player, Unit 4, Bentalls Ind. Estate, Colchester Rd, Maldon, Essex CM9 7NW

Hockey Field, Pat Ward, Green Crest, Silver Hill, Perranwell Station, Truro, Cornwall, TR3 7LR

World Hockey, International Hockey Federation, Avenue des Arts1, (BTE 5) B1040 Bruxelles, Belgium.

Videos of matches are legion but the best coaching video, in my view, is the Slazenger Coaching Video, available from the Hockey Association Coaching Office. There is also an Australian video on coaching, of excellent value and quality.

Finally, courses for coaches - not only for qualifications but for improvement - are run regionally and details are easily obtained from the appropriate Coaching Office. I do strongly commend these courses which are often staffed by the very best coaches in the land. Try to arrange that your club, in its Youth Policy programme, puts some money towards the cost.

The Youth Policy programme I've left, like all good things, to the last. It is vital that you help yourself and the players by trying to ensure that your input is part of the club infrastructure and remembering that no one is indispensable. In existence now for over a year, if you become ill, the Youth Development Policy should be able to take over your coaching. I strongly commend this to you, as it's always a pity to see hard work go to waste... work which, remember, is making a vital contribution to the future of the game and sport in general!

RULES OF THE GAME

Rules of the Game

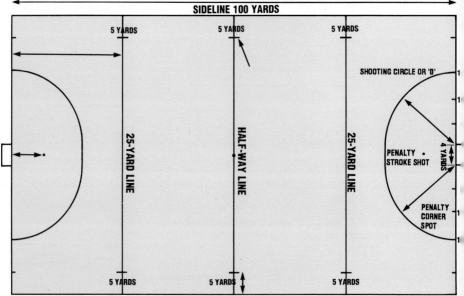

The Pitch Simplified

A diagram of the standard pitch is drawn complete but only to help you make decisions about the small-team games already discussed. **Coaches should see a pitch as areas of play.**

It's obvious that you need a big pitch for eleven-a-side but half a pitch is very suitable for seven players versus seven, mini-hockey, six-a-side and five-a-side. A quarter-size pitch can be used for four- and three-a-side. If you play across half a pitch you have a 60 yards by 50 area, and across a quarter 60 yards by 25. You can, of course, have several small-team games going simultaneously which prevents the common fault when coaching of having too many players who are not tired, watching.

Also as discussed in Chapter 5 you can use a particular area, say the right wing, for your two-versus-one player practices.

The Rules Simplified

It is beyond the scope of this book to go into great detail about the rules but you can obtain a rule book as outlined later in this chapter. It is often more helpful to look for comments on the rules.

Some simple guidelines

• **When is a 16-yard hit given?** When the ball crosses the goal line, off an attacker's stick or a defender's if outside the 25-yard area. Free hits given for offences by the attack, nearer than 16 yards to the goal line may be taken from the 16-yard line.

• **When is a free hit given?** For a breach of the rules other than penalty corners or strokes. When given less than five yards from the circle, both teams must be five yards from the ball and taker, but elsewhere only the opponents must be five yards from the free hit.

• **When is a corner given?** When the ball goes over the goal line having last touched the stick of a defender within the 25-yard area, and the touch is unintentional!

• **When is a penalty corner given?**

(i) For any deliberate offence by a defender within the 25-yard area but outside the circle;

(ii) For any unintentional infringement within the circle by a defender

(iii) For a deliberate playing of the ball behind the goal line by a defender, within the 25-yard area.

• **When is a hit-in given?** When the whole of the ball has crossed the whole of the side line, one of the opposite team can push or hit the ball after it is stationary on the line. Only the team defending the hit-in need be at least 5 yards from the ball.

• **When is a penalty stroke given?** (i) For any and all intentional breaches of the rules inside the circle by a defender;

(ii) If an unintentional breach of the rules has prevented a likely goal from being scored.

NB If a goalkeeper breaches the rules at a penalty stroke, a penalty goal is awarded even though the ball has not crossed the goal line.

• **When is a bully given?**
(i) After an accident or injury has occurred;
(ii) If the ball has been lodged in goalkeeper's equipment;
(iii) After other stoppages not involving free-hits. From the 1989 season players do not have to be on-side, and the bully cannot occur nearer than 16 yards to the goal line.
NB In the rule books corners and sideline hit-ins are all covered within Rule 17:' Ball Outside Field of Play' since they are all varieties of free hit. I deliberately use terms like corner and hit-in because they are in common usage and are more descriptive for coaching purposes.

The Important Rules - a Coaching Viewpoint

1. The prohibition of interfering with the body or stick of an opponent, in other words not playing the ball, at any time during the tackle. Coaches must be strict at all times on this one as it leads to loss of temper and generally heats up the game in the wrong way. In my opinion it is the worst-applied rule in hockey, partly because it's difficult to spot by umpires who don't move well.

A word of advice is always to umpire properly because, if you joke, the players will tend to fool about and if you are going to ignore the 'foot' rule then say so at an early stage. Youngsters don't mind what the rules are as long as you stick to them!
2. Obstruction. Just as stick interference is an example of bad play in the tackle, so obstruction is another one. We have taught the player how to move the ball from left to right to deliberately reduce obstruction, which is the placing of any part of the body between ball and opponent. You can make the concept easier for youngsters by explaining that one is not allowed to shield the ball, as in soccer, and that one should always turn back to one's own goal to avoid obstruction. Do not use the word 'turning' because this means that you will inhibit the skill, already described, of controlling the ball from behind.

Two cases of obstruction

Insist, also, that defenders who think that they can get 'up the back' of an attacker make a genuine attempt to play the ball, not simply hit the attacker across the shoulder blades with a stick! **NB** There's not much point in being fussy about 'foot' in practice especially in the early stages. Most youngsters are trying to get them out of the way and it's difficult for them even if they are footballers!

Off-side in training games or practices is also irrelevant. It simply creates yet another stoppage, like the foot rule. If you are over-fussy there will be a lot of stopping and starting which is very frustrating for a young learner. Remember what you are doing: teaching hockey within a framework of the rules.

3.Control at the penalty corner. A rule which will be necessary to apply since it is always strictly observed. The ball must be stopped, that is, stationary, before a shot at goal, which is a propulsion of the ball towards the goal (no matter what the speed). Some umpires blow the moving ball before the shot which is incorrect, but this rule affects a skill so it is important to remember it. The same applies to the rules on penalty strokes which are clearly explained in the rule book. It is very galling to have a good penalty stroke disallowed on a technicality.

Otherwise the rules are straightforward but I ought to issue a few warnings:
• Never let players argue with an umpire
• Insist on the highest disciplinary standard from the outset. A stick is a lethal weapon and wild behaviour cannot be tolerated.
• If using local rules, explain them first
• Do not allow players to wear dangerous items like watches and jewellery.

Mini-hockey rules

The rules for mini-hockey are obtainable from the Hockey Association Coaching Office but it is essentially a seven-versus-seven game with few rules and played on half a pitch. There are national competitions at Under-13 and Under-11 levels, but putting on such a tournament (say using 'A' and 'B' squads of nine each) is a good way to cement what you have done in training (see Chapter 10).

RULES OF THE GAME

THE FOLLOWING ARE SELECTED EXTRACTS FROM THE RULES AS ISSUED UNDER THE AUTHORITY OF THE HOCKEY RULES BOARD.

10. TO START OR RE-START THE GAME

(a) To start the game, re-start it after half-time and after each goal scored, a "pass-back" shall be played at the centre of the field. The pass-back for the start of the game shall be made by a player of the team which did not make a choice of ends (See Rule 2(a)), and after half-time by a player of the opposing team and after a goal has been scored, by a player of the team against whom the goal has been awarded. The pass-back, which may be pushed or hit, must not be directed over the centre line.

At the moment when the pass-back is taken, no player of the opposing team shall be within 5 yards of the ball and all players of both teams other than the player making the pass-back must be in their own half of the field.

If a striker hit at but miss the ball, the pass-back still has to be taken.

After taking the pass-back, the striker shall not play the ball again nor remain or approach within playing distance until it has been touched or played by another player of either team.

Time wasting shall not be permitted.

(b)(i) To re-start the game in accordance with Rule 7(f), Rule 12.III, Rule 12. Penalties 4 or Rule 18(b)(i) a bully shall be played on a spot to be

chosen by the umpire in whose half of the ground the incident occurred.
(b)(ii) To bully, a player of each team shall stand squarely facing the side-lines, each with his own back-line on his right. The ball shall be placed on the ground between the two players. Each player shall tap with his stick, first the ground between the ball and his own back-line, and then, with the flat face of the stick, his opponent's stick, over the ball, three times alternately, after which one of these two players shall play the ball with his stick to put it into play.
(iii) Until the ball is in play, all other players shall not stand within 5 yards of the ball.
(iv) A bully shall not be played within 16 yards of the back-line or goal line.

PENALITES
1. For a breach of Rule 10(a) a free hit shall be awarded to the opposing team.
2. For a breach of Rule 10(b)(iii) the bully shall be played again.

3. For persistent breaches of Rule 10(b)(ii) and (b)(iii) the umpire may award a free hit to the opposing team; or, for such breaches in the circle by a defender, a penalty corner.

GUIDANCE FOR PLAYERS AND UMPIRES
10. TO START OR RE-START THE GAME
(a) At the "pass back", the ball shall not be raised intentionally. The player taking the "pass back" shall not be penalised if the ball lifts slightly off the ground as long as the intention of play along the ground is clear.

(b)(ii)only the flat face of the stick may be used during the bully and

contact must take place over the ball. Much obstruction will be prevented if the two players are made to stand sqaure, not moving their feet until the ball is in play.
(iii) There is no requirement for players to be nearer their own back-line or goal-line than the ball is.
(iv) The umpire shall choose the spot in accordance with Rule 10(b)(i) and 10(b)(iv).

11. SCORING A GOAL
(a) A goal is scored when the whole ball, having been hit or deflected by the stick of an attacker whilst in the circle and not having gone outside the circle, passes completely over the goal-line between the goal-posts and under the cross-bar - except in circumstances detailed in Rule 15(e) and 15(i), when a goal may not be awarded, and in circumstances detailed in Rule 16 Penalty 1, when a goal may be awarded. It is immateral if the ball subsequently touch, be played by one or more defenders. If, during the game, the goal-posts and/ or cross-bar become displaced, and the ball pass completely over the goal-line at a point which, in the umpire's opinion, be between where the goal posts and/or under where the cross-bar, respectively, should have been, a goal shall be awarded.

(b) The team scoring the greater number of goals shall be the winner.

GUIDANCE FOR PLAYERS AND UMPIRES
11. SCORING A GOAL
The ball must be inside the circle when hit by an attacker (although he himself may be outside). If it is hit within the circle and then touches the

RULES OF THE GAME

stick or person of a defender or defenders before crossing the goal-line, a goal is scored.

Should the ball be hit from outside the circle by an attacker and be diverted between the posts by a defender who is in or outside the cricle within the 25-yard area, a corner should be given.

Note:
(i) the lines are part of the circle
(ii) the whole ball must cross the goal-line before a goal is scored.

After a stopppage of play inside the circle the ball must again be hit from inside the circle by the stick of an attacker, before a goal can be scored.

12. CONDUCT OF PLAY

I A player shall not:

(a) play the ball with the rounded side of the stick.

(b) take part in or interfere with the game unless he has his own stick in his hand, nor change his stick for the purpose of taking part in the game under Rules 14, 15, 16 and 17.

   "Own stick" means the stick with which the player began to play, or any stick that he legitimately substitutes for it.

(o) raioe hio otiok in a mannor that io dangerous, intimidating or hampering to another player when approaching, attempting to play, playing or stopping the ball. A ball above the height of a player's shoulder shall not be played or played at by any part of the stick. (For goalkeepers see Rule 12.II(c).)

(d) stop the ball with his hand or catch it. (For goal-keepers see Rule 12.II(c)).

(THERE IS NOTHING IN THIS RULE WHICH PREVENTS A PLAYER USING HIS HAND TO PROTECT HIMSELF FROM A DANGEROUSLY RAISED BALL).

(e) hit wildly into an opponent or play or raise or kick the ball in such a way as to be dangerous in itself, or likely to lead to dangerous play or play the ball intentionally into an opponent's foot, leg or body.

(f) stop or deflect the ball on the ground or in the air with any part of the body TO HIS OR HIS TEAM'S ADVANTAGE (save as provided for in Rule 12.II(c).)

(g) deliberately raise the ball from a HIT, except for a shot at goal.

(h) deliberately raise the ball so that it will fall into the circle.

(i) use the foot or leg to support the stick in order to resist an opponent.

(j) kick, pick up, throw, carry or propel the ball in any manner or direction except with the stick. (But see guidance 12.I(f), 12.I(i) and Rule 12.II(c).)

(k) hit, hook, hold, strike at or interfere with an opponent's stick.

(l) charge, kick, shove, trip, strike at or personally handle an opponent or his clothing.

(m) obstruct by running between an opponent and the ball nor interpose himself or his stick as an obstruction.

II A player may:

(a) play the ball only with the flat side of his stick which includes that part of the handle above the flat side.

(b) tackle from the left of an opponent provided that he play the ball without

catch it. (For goal-keepers see Rule 12.II(c)).

previous interference with the stick or person of his opponent. (See Rule 12.I particularly (k) (l) (m).)

(c) If he is a goal-keeper and the ball is inside his circle be allowed - contrary to the provisions of Rule 12.1(c)(d)(f) and (j) - to kick the ball, stop it with any part of his body including his hand and stop it with his stick above his shoulder, unless dangerous. No penalty shall be incurred if when stopping a shot at goal, the ball rebound off any part of the goalkeeper's body or his stick. (See Guidance 12.I(j)).

III

(a) if the ball become lodged in one of the pads of a goalkeeper or in the clothing of any player or umpire the umpire shall stop the game and re-start it by a bully on the spot where the incident occurred (subject to Rule 10(b)(iv)).

(b) If the ball strike an umpire the game shall continue.

IV *MISCONDUCT*

ROUGH OR DANGEROUS PLAY, TIME-WASTING, DELIBERATE BREACHES OF ANY RULE, OR ANY OTHER BEHAVIOUR WHICH IN THE UMPIRE'S OPINION AMOUNTS TO MISCONDUCT, SHALL NOT BE PERMITTED.

PENALTIES

1.*Outside the circle.*
A free hit shall be awarded to the opposing team. An umpire shall award a penalty corner for an offence by any defender in his own 25 yards

area, when, in the umpire's opinion, the offence was deliberate.

2. *Inside the circle - by an attacker.*
A free hit shall be awarded to the defending team.

3. *Inside the circle - by a defender.*
For a breach inside the circle by a defender a penalty corner shall be awarded or a penalty stroke if, in the umpire's opinion, Rule 16(a) applies.

4. *Inside and Outside the circle.*
For a simultaneous breach of this Rule by two opponents, the umpire shall order a bully to be played on the spot where the breach occurred (subject to Rule 10(b)(iv).)

5. *Inside and Outside the circle.*
For rough or dangerous play or misconduct, in addition to awarding the appropriate penalty, the umpire may:
(i) warn the offending player(s) which may also be indicated by showing a green card.
(ii) suspend him temporarily for not less than five minutes which may also be indicated by showing a yellow card.
(iii) suspend him from further participation in the game which may also be indicated by showing a red card.

A temporarily suspended player shall remain behind his own goal or in such other places as designated before the game, until allowed by the umpire by whom he was suspended, to resume play; when necessary changing ends at the start of the second half of the game.

GUIDANCE FOR PLAYERS AND UMPIRES
12. CONDUCT OF PLAY.

I(a) If the ball hits the back of the stick and no advantage result, no offence has taken place.

I(c) **Sticks**
A penalty stroke should be given when a defender (who is not the goal-keeper) has saved a probable goal on his stick above his shoulder.

Umpires should penalise and warn any player who lifts his stick over the head of an opponent. This type of action often leads to injuries and is accordingly dangerous play.

I(e) **Dangerous Play.**
This rule is intended to prevent injury to players and umpires. Umpires should be very firm in penalising dangerous play. A player may not deliberately raise the ball from a HIT except for a shot at goal. A rising ball is dangerous when it causes legitimate evasive action on the part of the players.

A player should be penalised who by raising the ball is guilty of or directly causes dangerous play. Hitting the ball whilst it is in the air is not permissible if the stroke is itself dangerous. The practice of lifting the ball from the ground and hitting it again while still in the air is prohibited.

I(f) **Stopping the Ball**
If the ball is lifted dangerously into an oncoming player who uses his hand to protect himself, he should not be penalised. If a penalty is given it should be against the player who raised the ball.

BEFORE PENALISING A BREACH INVOLVING THE STOPPING OF THE BALL WITH SOME PART OF THE BODY THE UMPIRE MUST BE SATISFIED THAT THE PLAYER CONCERNED USED HIS BODY.

(i) BY MOVING INTO THE LINE OF THE BALL.
(ii) BY SO POSITIONING HIMSELF THAT HIS INTENTION TO STOP THE BALL IN SUCH A MANNER WAS CLEAR.
(iii) BY MAKING NO EFFORT TO AVOID BEING HIT.

It is not necessarily an offence if the ball strike the foot or body of a player.

I(g) Not every ball entering the circle off the ground is forbidden - only those deliberately raised which fall directly into the circle.
A ball which bounces into the circle or a hit entering the circle off the ground must be judged solely on grounds of danger.
A ball slightly raised over an opponent's stick or goal-keeper's body when on the ground is permitted, but must be judged according to danger.

I(i) **Propelling the Ball**
(i) the ball must not be carried forward in any way by the body.
(ii) a player should not be penalised for a rebound when the ball has been propelled straight at him from close quarters by an opponent.

RULES OF THE GAME

(iii) Goal-keepers should not be penalised when using their hands or kicking or propelling the ball with their feet or pads unless the propelled ball is considered either dangerous or likely to lead to dangerous play. The act of touching/deflecting the ball over the cross-bar or around a goalpost by hand is permitted unless dangerous.

I(j) Stick Interference
Hooking and striking at sticks should be strictly penalised.

Should a player slash wildly at the ball and hit an opponent or his stick instead, he should be penalised. A player may not throw his stick at the ball.

I(k)(l) Body Interference and Obstruction
Subject to the "advantage rule" umpires should be particularly strict on obstruction and other forms of interference dealt with in this Rule. It should be noted that obstruction does not necessarily depend on the distance from the ball of the players concerned.

A player, even if in possession of the ball, may not interpose his body as an obstruction to an opponent. A change of direction by a half-turn of the body with this result may amount to obstruction. It should be noted, however, that even a complete turn does not constitute a breach unless an opponent has thereby been obstructed in an attempt to play the ball.

Obstruction occurs at hit-ins and should be watched for carefully.

A player must not interpose any part of his body or his stick as an obstruction between his opponent and the ball. Watch too for third party interference i.e. a player interposing himself between his opponent and the ball so that a fellow player has an opportunity to clear or play the ball.

Other names for these offences are: shadow-obstruction, shepherding, blocking out or even as a general term "close-marking".

II(c) The Goal-keeper.
A goal-keeper is not allowed to strike at the ball with his hand, or stick it out with his body. (See Guidance 12.I(j)). Umpires are disposed to be too lenient towards breaches of the Rules by goal-keepers.

The more usual breaches are running between an opponent and the ball when it is about to go behind, opening the legs to let the ball go through when an opponent is within striking distance and making a wild stroke at the ball when clearing. The goal-keeper must not be allowed further privileges than those given by this Rule.

Goal-keepers are not permitted to kick dangerously. (See 12.1(e)).

PENALTIES

The penalties for rough and dangerous play, misconduct, deliberate breaches of the Rules, or time-wasting, should be noted carefully, and the appropriate penalty awarded.
Persistent breaches of the Rules may

suitably be dealt with under this Rule. If rough or dangerous play becomes prevalent, a word of caution to the offender(s) should effectively prevent the game getting out of hand. For those breaches of the Rule inside the circle Rule 16 should also be taken into consideration.

Nothing in these Rules prevents a suspended player joining his team during the half-time interval but he should return to the suspended players' position on resumption of the second half of play unless his suspension has been ended.

13. OFF-SIDE.

(a) AT THE MOMENT WHEN THE BALL IS PLAYED a player of the same team as the pusher or striker is in an offside position if he be in his opponent's 25 yards area unless:
he be behind the ball
or
there be at least two opponents nearer to their own back-line or goal-line than he is.

For the purpose of this Rule, a player of either team shall be deemed to be on the field of play even though he be outside the side-line or behind the back-line or goal-line.

(b) A player who is an off-side position shall not play or attempt to play the ball or gain any advantage for his team or influence the play of an opponent.

PENALTY.
A free hit shall be awarded to the defending team.

GUIDANCE FOR PLAYERS AND UMPIRES
13. OFF-SIDE

The question of whether a player is off-side is governed by WHERE HE WAS AT THE MOMENT WHEN THE BALL WAS PLAYED BY A PLAYER OF THE SAME TEAM not where he is when he received the ball. The umpire must always have this in mind otherwise he may easily give a wrong decision. The act of 'playing' the ball includes when a player of the same team is dribbling the ball.

A player in an off-side position whether on or off the field SHOULD NOT BE PENALISED UNLESS he influence the play of an opponent or gain some advantage from his off-side position. A player who is level with the ball is off-side.

A player cannot be off-side if:

(a) he is nearer the 25 yards line than the ball is at the time it is played by a player of the same team.

there are at least two opponents nearer to their own back-line than he is at the moment when the ball is played by a player of the same team.

If a player is off-side, he is not automatically put on-side by returning to his own side of his opponents' 25 yards line to play the ball.

A whole line of forwards having outdistanced the defence and only having the goal-keeper in front of them could pass and re-pass to each other without being off-side as long as they keep behind the ball.

(b) A player who is left off-side after

making a previous shot should not be penalised if he is trying to get back on-side, unless he is obstructing or distracting any opponent.

14. FREE HIT

(a) A free hit shall be taken on the spot where the breach occurred except that:
(i) **for a breach by an attacker within the circle** it shall be taken:
EITHER
from any spot within that circle
OR
from any spot within 16 yards of the inner edge of the defending team's back-line or goal-line on a line drawn through the place where the breach occurred and parallel to the side-line.
(ii) **for a breach by an attacker outside the circle but within 16 yards of the defending team's back-line** it shall be taken from any spot within 16 yards of the inner edge of the defending team's back-line on a line drawn through the place where the breach occurred and parallel to the sideline.

(b) The ball shall be stationary and the striker shall push or hit it. The ball must be moved and shall not be raised intentionally or in such a way as to be dangerous in itself, or likely to lead to dangerous play.

(c) At the moment when the free hit is taken, no player of the opposing team shall remain within 5 yards of the ball. However, for a free hit to the attacking team within 5 yards of the circle, players of both teams, except the striker, shall be at least 5 yards from the ball. Should the umpire consider

that a player is standing within 5 yards of the ball in order to gain time, the free hit shall not be delayed.

(d) If the striker hit at but miss the ball, provided that Rule 12.I(c) has not been contravened, the free hit still has to be taken.

(c) After taking the free hit, the striker shall not play the ball again nor remain or approach within playing distance until it has been touched or played by another player of either team.

PENALTIES

1. *Inside the circle.*

A penalty corner or penalty stroke shall be awarded to the attacking team.

2. *Outside the circle.*
A free hit shall be awarded to the opposing team. An umpire shall award a penalty corner for an offence by any defender in his own 25 yards area, when in the umpire's opinion, the offence was deliberate.

GUIDANCE FOR PLAYERS AND UMPIRES
14. FREE HIT.

The free hit must be taken from the right place and the ball must be stationary. If a player taking a free hit gains extra advantage by taking the free hit from the wrong place, he should be penalised.

A free hit in the circle may be taken from any place within the circle.

RULES OF THE GAME

Should there be any unnecessary delay by the players of the offending side in observing the 5-yards distance. Rule, the umpire need not order the hit to be taken again but 14. should warn offending players. The application of Rule 12, Penalty 5, should be considered if an opponent knocks the ball away after a free hit has been awarded.

(b) At the free hit, the ball shall not be raised intentionally. The player taking the free hit shall not be penalised if the ball lifts off the ground as long as the intention to play along the ground is clear. Simply touching the ball with the stick is not considered to be a hit; the ball must move from its original position.

15. PENALTY CORNER

(a) A penalty corner shall be awarded to the opposing team if, in the umpire's opinion:
(i) there has been an INTENTIONAL breach of Rules 12, 14 or 17 inside the 25 yards area but outside the circle by a player of the defending team.
OR
(ii) an UNINTENTIONAL breach of Rule 12, 14 or 17.II(b) inside the circle by a player of the defending team.
OR
(iii) For persistent breaches of Rule 10(b)(ii) or (b)(iii) in the circle by a defender.

(b) A player of the attacking team shall push or hit the ball from a spot on the back-line not less than 10 yards from the goal-post, on

whichever side of the goal the attacking team prefers. The player concerned is not required to be wholly inside or outside the field of play when taking the corner.
The ball shall not be raised intentionally but the hit shall not be penalised if the ball lifts off the ground without causing danger or appearing likely to lead to dangerous play.

(c) (i) At the moment when such push or hit is made, no other player shall be within 5 yards of the ball.
The rest of the attacking team shall be in the field of play with both sticks and feet outside the circle.
Not more than five of the defending team shall stand with both sticks and feet behind their own goal-line or back-line. The rest of the defending team shall be beyond the centre-line.

(ii) In the event of the defending goal-keeper being incapacitated or suspended, his team captain shall immediately nominate another goal-keeper. This goal-keeper shall be permitted to put on without undue delay, protective equipment. Under the provisions of this Rule, a goal-keeper may also remove his headgear face mask and/or his gauntlet gloves (see Rule 9(b).)

(d) Until the ball be pushed or hit no attacker shall enter the circle, nor shall a defender cross the goal-line, back-line or centre-line.

(e)(i) No shot at goal shall be made from a penalty corner until the ball be stopped or come to rest on the ground or touch the stick or person of

a defender. The defending goal-keeper shall remain on his feet until the first shot at goal has been made.
(ii) If the first shot at goal is a HIT the ball shall not cross the goal-line at a height higher than the back-board/side-boards (18 inches) unless it has touched the stick or person of a defender.
(iii)If the ball travels beyond 5 yards from the outer edge of the circle line, the penalty corner is ended and the special provisions mentioned in (i) and (ii) no longer apply.

(f) The player taking the penalty corner hit or push from the back-line shall not, after striking the ball, play the ball again nor approach or remain within playing distance of the ball until it has been touched or played by another player of either team.

(g) If the striker of the penalty corner hit at or push at but miss the ball, the penalty corner still has to be taken.

(h) No goal shall be scored directly by the player taking the penalty corner hit or push from the back-line, even if the ball be played into goal by a defender.

PENALTIES.

1. *For a breach of Rule 15(c)(i) or 15(d) viz:*

Attacker(s) entering the circle or defender(s) crossing the goal-line, back-line or centre-line too soon or coming within 5 yards of the ball too soon - the penalty corner may, at the discretion of the umpire, be taken again.

2. *For persistent breaches of Rule 15(b)(i) or 15(c) by the attackers -* The umpire may award a free hit.

3. *For persistent breaches of Rule 15(b)(i) or 15(c) by the defenders -* The umpire may award a penalty stroke.

4. *For an unintentional breach of Rule 15(e)(i) by the goalkeeper -* The penalty corner may, at the discretion of the umpire, be taken again.

5. *For intentional or persistent breaches of Rule 15(e)(i) by the goalkeeper -* The umpire shall award a penalty stroke.

6. *For any other breach of Rule 15 -* A free hit shall be awarded to the defending team.

GUIDANCE FOR PLAYERS AND UMPIRES
15. PENALTY CORNER.

(c)(i) Both teams should be correctly positioned.
(ii) The returning incapacitated or temporarily suspended goal-keeper is permitted to put on, without undue delay, protective equipment.

(d) The umpire has the right to order the penalty corner to be taken again if a defender crosses the goal-line, or back-line or the centre line before the ball is hit. This power should, however, be used with discretion. It is often to the disadvantage of the attacker to stop the game when the corner has been well hit, well stopped and resulted in the attacker being in a good position to shoot.

(e) Although the first HIT must not cross the goal-line above a height of 18 inches, there is no limit to the height of a push, flick or scoop or of any subsequent stroke, subject always to there being no danger. Nor is there any limit to the height of a HIT before it crosses the line subject always to there being no danger.

(f) The ball must be stopped. The ball may be deflected or passed one or more times by the attacking players, but it must be stopped or come to a stop at some time inside or outside within 5 yards of the circle before a shot at goal is made.

(i) If the ball has not previously been touched by a defender, or has not been stopped on the ground, a flying hit following a pass or deflection from one attacker to another, should be penalised as a breach of this Rule. "Directly" means before another player of the attacking team has played the ball.

16. PENALTY STROKE

(a) A penalty stroke shall be awarded to the opposing team if that team has possession of the opportunity to gain possession of the ball in the circle and, in the opinion of the umpire:
(i) there has been an INTENTIONAL breach of Rules 12, 14 or 17.II(a)(v) inside the circle by a player of the defending team.
          OR
(ii) a goal would probably have been scored had an UNINTENTIONAL breach of Rule 12 inside the circle by a player of the defending team not occurred.

(iii) Rules 15(c)(i) and/or 15(d) are persistently breached by the defenders.

(b) (i) The penalty stroke shall be a push, flick or scoop stroke taken from a spot 7 yards in front of the centre of the goal by a player of the attacking team and defended by the goal-keeper of the opposing team on the field at the time the breach occurred.
In the event of the defending goal-keeper being incapacitated or suspended, his team captain shall immediately nominate another goal-keeper. This goal-keeper shall be permitted to put on or remove, without undue delay, protective equipment. Under the provisions of this Rule, a goal-keeper may also remove his face mask, headgear and/or his gauntlet gloves (see Rule 9(b)).
(ii) Whichever stroke is used, the ball may be raised to any height.
(iii) During the taking of a penalty stroke all the other players of both teams shall be beyond the nearer 25-yards line, and shall not influence or attempt to influence the conduct of the penalty stroke.

(c) (i) The attacking player shall not take the penalty stroke until the umpire, having satisfied himself that both defender and attacker are ready, has indicated that he shall do so by blowing his whistle.
(ii) When taking the stroke the attacker shall stand close to and behind the ball and shall be permitted in making the stroke to take one stride forward. Dragging or lifting the rear foot is not a breach of this Rule, provided that it does not pass the front foot before the ball is moved.

(iii) The attacker shall touch the ball once only and thereafter shall not approach either the ball or the goal-keeper.

(d) (i) The goal-keeper shall stand on the goal-line. After the player taking the stroke and the goal-keeper are in position and the umpire has blown his whistle, the goal-keeper shall not leave the goal-line or move either of his feet until the ball has been played.
(ii) The usual privileges of the goal-keeper shall be allowed to him, but he shall not be allowed to delay the taking of the stroke by making unnecessary changes or modifications of clothing. If the ball be caught and held by the goal-keeper the Penalty Stroke is ended. (See also clause (e)(ii).) He shall not be penalised, if in stopping a shot at goal, the ball, in the umpire's opinion, merely rebounds off his body, stick or his hand.
(iii) If any deliberate action by the striker prior to striking the ball, induces the goal-keeper to move either of his feet, or, if the striker feints at striking the ball, the striker shall be penalised.

(e) If, as a result of the penalty stroke
(i) the whole ball pass completely over the goal-line between the goal-posts and under the cross-bar, a goal is scored.
(ii) the ball should come to rest inside the circle, be lodged in the goal-keeper's pads, be caught by the goal-keeper, or pass outside the circle, in all cases, the penalty stroke is ended. Unless a goal has

been scored or awarded, the game shall be re-started by a free hit to be taken by a defender from a spot in front of the centre of the goal and 16 yards from the inner edge of that line.

(f) All time taken between the award of a penalty stroke and resumption of play shall be added to the time of play.

PENALTIES

1. For a breach of any Rule by the goal-keeper which prevents a goal from being scored, a goal shall be awarded to the opposing team. (See Penalty 3 below).

2. For a breach of any Rule by an attacker, the game shall be re-started with a free hit to be taken by a defender from a spot in front of the centre of the goal-line and 16 yards from the inner edge of that line.

3. For a breach of clause (b)(iii) or (d)(i) the umpire may order the stroke to be taken again.

GUIDANCE FOR PLAYERS AND UMPIRES
16. PENALTY STROKE

(a) Note the cases in which this may be awarded, and that it shall be awarded if, in the umpire's opinion, an intentional breach of rules 12, 14 or 17.II(a) (v) has been committed inside the circle even though it may seem to the umpire improbable that, but for the breach a goal could have been scored. The intentional breach must be against a player who either has possession of the ball or the

opportunity to gain possession of the ball.
It should be particularly noted that this penalty is intended to meet offences which may materially affect the game, when a more severe penalty than a penalty corner is necessary, and it should be applied accordingly by umpires.
It is not always easy for an umpire to decide whether a breach is intentional or not, but a distinction should be made between committing a breach of the Rules that is entirely forbidden, such as charging, and a breach which is the result of an attempt to do something lawful. A defender must show by his actions that he has tried to prevent fouling an attacker e.g. charging into a player about to shoot from a favourable position should invariably be regarded as intentional for the purpose of this Rule.
If a goal-keeper falls on or beside the ball in front of goal, an award of a penalty stroke would be appropriate in most cases where the opponents thereby have no fair view of the ball or opportunity to play the ball.

(b)(i) A goal-keeper may put on or take off his mask, headgear and/or his gauntlet gloves. If the attacking goal-keeper takes the stroke, he may also remove his mask, headgear and/or gauntlet gloves. Equally a substitute goal-keeper shall be permitted to put on without undue delay protective equipment.

(b)(iii) For a breach of Rule 16(b)(iii) by an attacker when a goal is scored or by a defender when no goal is scored, the Penalty Stroke may be taken again.

(c)(i) If the attacker takes the stroke before the umpire has blown his whistle, the game shall be re-started by a free hit to the defending team.

If there is any unreasonable delay or misconduct by either a defender or an attacker in carrying out any of the provisions of this Rule, the umpire may treat such action as misconduct (Rule 12 IV) and deal with it accordingly.

For a breach of Rules 16(c)(i) and (d)(iii), a free hit from 16 yards from the centre of the goal shall be awarded.

17. BALL OUTSIDE FIELD OF PLAY.

When the whole ball passes completely over the back-line and no goal is scored, or over the side-line, it is out of play and the game shall be re-started as in Rules 17.I and 17.II.

I Over side-line.
(a) When the whole ball passes completely over the side-line, it or another ball, shall be placed on the line at the spot at which it crossed the side-line. The ball shall be pushed or hit without undue delay by a player of the team opposed to the player who last touched it in play. This player is not required to be wholly inside or outside the side-line when making his push or hit.

(b) The ball shall be stationary and the striker shall push or hit it. The ball must be moved and shall not be raised intentionally or in such a way as to be dangerous in itself or likely to

lead to dangerous play.

(c) At the moment when the push or hit is taken no player of the opposing team shall be within 5 yards of the ball. If any player of the opposing team be within 5 yards of the ball, the umpire may require the push or hit to be taken again. If, however, in the umpire's opinion, a player of the opposing team remain within 5 yards of the ball to gain time, the push or hit shall not be delayed.

(d) If the striker hit at but miss the ball, provided that Rule 12.I(c) has not been contravened, the push or hit still has to be taken.

(e) After taking a push or hit the player shall not play the ball again, nor remain or approach within playing distance of the ball until it has been touched or played by another player of either team.

PENALTY

For any breach of this Rule, a free hit shall be awarded to the opposing team.

II Over back-line.
(a) By an attacker.
(i) When the ball passes completely over the opponents' back-line by or off one of the attacking team and no goal is scored, it or another ball shall be placed on a spot opposite the place where it crossed the back-line and not more than 16 yards from the inner edge of that line. The ball shall be pushed or hit without undue delay by one of the defending team.
(ii) The ball shall be stationary and

the striker shall push or hit it. The ball must be moved and shall not be raised intentionally or in such a way as to be dangerous in itself or likely to lead to dangerous play.
(iii) No player of the opposing team shall be within 5 yards of the ball when the push or hit is taken.
(iv) If the striker hit at but miss the ball, provided that Rule 12.I(c) has not been contravened, the push or hit still has to be taken.
(v) After taking the push or hit, the striker shall not play the ball again nor remain nor approach within playing distance of the ball until it has been touched or played by another player of either team

(b) *By a defender.*
(i) When the ball, in the umpire's opinion is sent unintentionally over his own back-line or goal-line by or off one of the defending team who is within his own 25 yards area, a push or hit shall be taken by the attacking team, unless a goal has been scored.

(a) The player shall push or hit the ball from a spot on the back-line within 5 yards of the corner flag nearer to the point where the ball crossed the back-line.

(b) The ball shall be stationary and the striker shall push or hit it. The ball must be moved and shall not be raised intentionally or in such a way as to be dangerous in itself or likely to lead to dangerous play.

(c) No player of the opposing team shall be within 5 yards of the ball when the push or hit is taken.

(d) If the striker hit at but miss the ball, provided that Rule 12.I(c) has not been contravened, the push or hit still has to be taken.

(e) After taking the push or hit, the striker shall not play the ball again nor remain or approach within playing distance of the ball until it has been touched or played by another player of either team.
(ii) When the ball, in the umpire's opinion is sent over his own back-line or goal-line by or off one of the defending team who is more than 25 yards from the back-line, the game shall be re-started by a push or hit by one of the defending team from a spot opposite the place where it crossed the back-line or goal-line and not more than 16 yards from the inner edge of that line.
(a) The ball shall be stationary and the striker shall push or hit it. The ball must be moved and shall not be raised intentionally or in such a way as to be dangerous in itself or likely to lead to dangerous play.
(b) No player of the opposing team shall be within 5 yards of the ball when the push or hit is taken.
(c) If the striker hit at but miss the ball, provided that Rule 12.I(c) has not been contravened, the push or hit still has to be taken.
(d) After taking the push or hit, the striker shall not play the ball again nor remain nor approach within playing distance of the ball until it has been touched or played by another player of either team.

PENALTIES

1. For a breach of this Rule by an attacker, a free hit shall be awarded to the defending team.

2. For a ball raised dangerously from a free hit within the circle by a defender, a penalty corner shall be awarded.

3. For an unintentional breach of this Rule by a defender outside the circle a free hit shall be awarded to the attacking team.

4. For an unintentional breach of this Rule inside the circle or for an intentional breach of this Rule by a defender within the 25 yards area but outside the circle, a penalty corner shall be awarded.

5. For an intentional breach of this Rule by a defender within the circle, a penalty stroke shall be awarded.

(iii) No player may deliberately play or deflect the ball over his own back-line or goal-line from an area enclosed by the 25 yards line, including the circle.

PENALTY
For a breach of this Rule, a penalty corner shall be awarded to the opposing team.

GUIDANCE FOR PLAYERS AND UMPIRES
17. BALL OUTSIDE FIELD OF PLAY.

17.1(a) When pushed or hit, the ball shall not be raised intentionally. The player taking the push or hit shall not be penalised if the ball lifts slightly off the ground as long as the intention to play along the ground is clear.

17.1(b) Simply touching the ball with the stick is not considered to be a hit.
A free hit to the defending team may be brought up to 16 yards from the back-line, if the breach was nearer to the back-line.
(See Rule 14(a)(ii)).
(See Guidance to Rule 14 on page 119-20).

II.(a)(ii)When pushed or hit, the ball shall not be raised intentionally. The player taking the push or hit shall not be penalised if the ball lifts slightly off the ground as long as the intention to play along the ground is clear.
Simply touching the ball with the stick is not considered to be a hit; the ball must move from its original position.
If the ball be hit by, or glance off, the stick or person of a defender over his own back-line or goal-line, note that the decision must, unless a goal be scored, be:

II(b)(i) A push or hit from the back-line if unintentionally from within his own 25-yards area.

II(b)(i)(a) Simply touching the ball with the stick is not considered to be a hit; the ball must move from its original position.
In deciding whether a push or hit from the back-line or a penalty corner should be awarded, the only point at issue is whether the hit or deflection was intentional or unintentional. The fact that, in sending the ball over the back-line a defender saves a goal must not influence an umpire in his decision.

17.II(b)(iii) The only point at issue is

whether the stroke or deflection was intentional or not. The fact that, in sending the ball over the back-line, a defender saves a goal must not influence an umpire in his decision.

The conduct of the penalty corner is described in Rule 15.

18. ACCIDENTS

(a) If a player or an umpire be incapacitated, the umpire or other umpire shall stop the game temporarily noting the time lost. (See Rule 3 (f).)

In either case, if a goal be scored before the game be stopped it shall be allowed if, in the umpire's opinion, it would have been scored had the accident not occurred.

(b) The umpire shall re-start the game as soon as possible, by:

(i) a bully (subject to Rule 10(b)(iv)) on a spot to be chosen by the umpire in whose half of the ground the accident occurred.
OR
(ii) the appropriate penalty when the accident was the result of a breach of the rules.
OR
(iii) the implementation of a decision given before the game was stopped.

(c) If the umpire concerned cannot continue, the other umpire shall re-start the game.

GUIDANCE FOR PLAYERS AND UMPIRES
18. ACCIDENTS

The umpire should see that an injured player leaves the field of play as soon as possible, unless medical reasons prohibit this action.

DEFINITIONS OF HOCKEY TERMINOLOGY

1. Playing the Ball
Playing the ball is stopping or moving the ball with the stick in any manner or, in the case of the goalkeeper, with the foot, hand or any part of the body.

2. A Stroke
A 'stroke' is executed when the ball has been moved by playing, striking or deflecting it.

3. A Hit
A 'hit' is a stroke with a swinging movement of the stick in order to increase the ball's speed.

4. A Push
A 'push' moves the ball along the ground by a pushing movement of the stick after the stick has been placed close to the stationary or rolling ball. When a push is made, both the ball and head of the stick are in contact with the ground.

5. The Flick
A 'flick' occurs when a stationary or rolling ball is pushed and, as a result, is raised off the ground.

6. The Scoop
A 'scoop' occurs when a stationary or nearly motionless ball is raised off the ground by means of a shovel-movement of the stick, after the head of the stick is placed slightly under the ball.

7. A Shot at Goal
Any stroke by an attacker within the circle towards goal.

8. Pass-Back
The pass-back is a push or hit not directed over the centre-line, which means the ball must be played either square or in any backward direction.

9. Playing Distance
Playing distance is in the distance within which a player is capable of playing the ball. The playing distance will depend upon the reach of the player involved.
If the Rules require players to remain beyond playing distance of the ball, the players are not allowed to play, approach or attempt to play the ball until it has been played or touched by another player of either team.

10. Persistent
If in the Rules the word 'persistent' is used, it means the first time and all subsequent times after a warning has been given for any particular breach.

RULES OF THE GAME

RULES OF HOCKEY - TECHNICAL INTERPRETATIONS

The Rules of Hockey leave much to the individual interpretation of the Umpire. By their very nature, such elements as dangerous play, the lifted ball and obstruction will depend upon the relevant position of other players. Although the Rules Book includes Guidance for Players and Umpires, it is thought that the following require further explanation to try to ensure more consistent interpretation by Umpires.

LIFTED BALL (Rule 12.1 (e))
The raised ball must be judged on its dangerous aspects at the spot from where the ball is played, during flight and where the ball lands. The breach of the Rules should be penalised on the spot where the danger occurs, not necessarily from where the ball was originally played.

(a) If the danger occurs at the place from where the ball has been played, the penalty must be taken from there.

(b) When the danger occurs at a place where the ball lands, the penalty must be taken from there.

(c) When the danger occurs during the flight of the ball, the penalty should be taken from the place from which the ball originally came.

The only exception would be if a player of either team behaved in an unnecessarily dangerous manner in the area of the flight of the ball.

The difference between the application of the penalties mentioned above from the application in the past, is that the ball need not be brought back to the place from where the ball had been played.

It is forbidden to deliberately raise the ball by any stroke so that it will fall directly into the circle. It is important to realise that not every ball entering the circle off the ground is forbidden.

A ball raised slightly over an opponent's stick or body whilst on the ground is permitted, subject as always to the raised ball not being dangerous or likely to lead to dangerous play.

A ball which bounces into the circle from a lofted stroke must be judged solely on its dangerous aspects. A hit entering the circle off the ground must also be judged according to the dangerous play rule.

RIGHTS OF THE GOALKEEPER (Rule 12)
If the goalkeeper propels the ball by his hand over the cross-bar or around a goal post, it is not a breach of Rule 12.1 (i). Propelling the ball by hand is only allowed as a reaction to hits, pushes, scoops or flicks at goal. Propelling a stationary ball by hand is not allowed and must be penalised according to the penalties in Rule 12.

MANUFACTURED FOUL/ INTENTIONAL BREACH (RULE 12)
Play is interrupted many times during a match for obstruction. Some of those interruptions result from breaches which have been manufactured, which means that the opponents have been forced into breaching unintentionally one of the Rules.

Such breaches must be penalised. To clarify obstruction:

When a player places himself or his stick between the ball and an opponent, it is an obstruction. When another player of the same team gains an advantage, it is called third party obstruction.

Obstruction usually concerns an active action by the player in question.

Forcing an opponent into an obstructive position, often emphasized by running into the opponent or by waving his stick over the opponent, are actions which must be penalised.

However, it must be remembered that for a player to be obstructed, that player must be:
(a) ATTEMPTING TO PLAY THE BALL, which means if the ball is on the ground so must be his stick. He must demonstrate a genuine attempt is being made to play the ball
(b) ATTEMPTING TO PLAY THE BALL from a position from which he can play it without first interfering with the opponent's stick or body.
The Guidance to Rule 12.1 (f) states: "It is not necessarily an offence if the ball strikes the foot or body of a player."

This emphasized the point that if the ball 'strikes' the foot, rather than the foot 'kicking the ball' there may be no breach of the Rules.

If a player of the opposing team was responsible, then there is no foul.

Rules 12.1 (e) says "A player shall not play the ball intentionally into an opponent's foot, leg or body." If he does then the Umpire may decide to let play go or penalise the offence with a free hit, or a penalty-corner if it is done by a defender in his own circle."

There are a number of occasions when players will intentionally breach the Rules to gain an advantage fro their team. Such occasions will include knocking the ball away after a free hit has been awarded, picking the ball up and carrying it away before returning it to the opposing team, playing the ball with the hand or above the shoulder with the stick. All intentional breaches must be penalised in accordance with the penalties set out in the rules. Strict action taken early in the game will usually result in non-repetition of the offence.

However, if such action doesn't get the required results, penalty 5(i) and (ii) should be activated. Only in exceptional circumstances should 5(iii) be used.

SUSPENSION OF PLAYERS (RULE 12)

In addition to the awarding of various penalties for breaches of the Rules, Umpires are provided with powers to warn and/or suspend players when circumstances justify. The Rules are clear that such powers are in addition

to existing penalties, not a substitution for them. It is important therefore that they should be used thoughtfully and have a clear purpose in mind.

Umpires must remember that if a card is used for an offence early in the game, they have set the precedent for the remainder of that game. It is important to be consistent so think carefully before using the card.

FREE HIT (Rule 14)

Rule 14(a) requires that a Free Hit shall be taken on the spot where the breach occurred (see Rule 14(a) for exceptions) and the ball shall be stationary before the push or hit is taken.

Regarding the right spot, Umpires must be a little lenient, but when a team gains an extra advantage by breaching the above Rule, a free hit must be awarded to the opposing team. Regarding the ball being stationary, there should be no leniency even to the extent of awarding a penalty-corner for persistent breaches of the Rule within the circle of 25 yard area.

It should be noted that the free hit has been taken when the ball undergoes some appreciable movement after the push or hit has been taken. Placing the stick on a stationary ball is not an execution of the free hit.

Umpires should remember that whilst players of the opposing team are required to be 5 yards from the ball when the push or hit is taken, they must be given sufficient time to do so

before they are penalised. The free hit does not have to be delayed until they are. Such action would be detrimental to the flow of the game. However, players of the opposing team who delay the taking of the free hit by whatever means - not withdrawing 5 yards, hitting the ball away, handling the ball before returning it to the opposing team, should be penalised as appropriate , more severely for persistent breaches.

Umpires should not penalise every free hit when the ball lifts slightly off the ground, so long as the intention to play along the ground is clear and the hit itself is not dangerous or leading to dangerous play.

PENALTY CORNER (RULE 15)

The Rule requires:

Not more than five of the defending team shall stand with both sticks and feet behind their own goal-line or back-line. The rest of the defending team shall be beyond the centre-line.

The following guidance may be helpful:

1. Before any hit or other stroke is played which results in the ball moving towards the goal, the ball must be stopped or come to rest on the ground either inside or outside the circle.

2. The ball must then be stationary, although it may be spinning on the spot which sometimes happens on artificial surfaces.

RULES OF THE GAME

3. There is no requirement that the ball must be stopped by the stick. It could just cease to move on its own.

4. It has been the practice in International Tournaments to require the first hit at goal at the penalty corner to be of a height lower than the top of the back-board or side-boards unless the ball has been deflected by the stick or body of a defender.

The 'first hit' is the first hit at a goal after the ball has been stopped regardless of the number of times the ball has been passed or deflected, provided it has not been played or touched the stick or body of a defender. If it has been, the dangerous play rule will apply.

If at any time during a penalty corner the ball goes 5 yards or more beyond the edge of the circle, the ball is deemed to be in normal field play and therefore only subject to the dangerous play rule.

Under these circumstances, there is no requirement for the ball to be stopped before a hit at goal is made. The first hit at goal under all other circumstances must enter the goal at a height lower than the top of the back-board or side-boards.

5. A first hit at goal which is higher than the backboard or side-boards must be penalised even if it touches one of them as the result of a deflection off the stick or body of a defender.

6. Every stroke following the first hit or other stroke remains subject to the Rules of dangerous play.

7. High flicks or scoop strokes are permitted at any time subject to the Rule governing dangerous play.

8. As long as there are players in the circle in front of goal, any high shot may be dangerous.

9. Special attention must be given to the breach by defenders of crossing the goal-line or back-line too early.

PENALTY STROKE (RULE 16)
A penalty stroke should be awarded when a defender commits a breach of the Rules inside the circle against a player of the opposing team who has possession of the ball or is likely to gain possession of the ball.

16 Yards Hit (Rule 17.11 (a))

The Rule requires that the push or hit may be taken up to 16 yards from the goal-line or back-line. Recently, players have been taking the push or hit nearer to 20 yards from the goal-line or back-line. This should not be permitted.

THIS BOOK HAS SHOWN THE IMPORTANT AND WIDE-RANGING ROLE OF THE COACH. IT HAS ALSO INDICATED THE KNOWLEDGE REQUIRED TO BE AN EFFECTIVE AND SUCCESSFUL COACH. THE SCOPE OF THIS BOOK CANNOT COVER EVERY TOPIC IN DETAIL, SO IF YOU HAVE DEVELOPED AN INTEREST IN SOME ASPECT OF COACHING SUCH AS MENTAL PREPARATION, FITNESS TRAINING OR THE PREVENTION OF INJURY, THE **NATIONAL COACHING FOUNDATION**, ESTABLISHED TO PROVIDE A SERVICE FOR SPORTS COACHES, RUNS COURSES, PRODUCES STUDY PACKS, BOOKS, VIDEOS AND OTHER RESOURCES ON MANY PERFORMANCE RELATED AREAS PARTICULARLY DESIGNED FOR THE PRACTISING COACH.

CONTACT THE **NATIONAL COACHING FOUNDATION** AT: 4 COLLEGE CLOSE, BECKETT PARK, LEEDS LS6 3QH. TELEPHONE: LEEDS (0532) 744802